D0030312

GOLD IN THE MAKING

GOLD
IN THE
MAKING

Ron Lee Davis
with
James D. Denney

THOMAS NELSON PUBLISHERS
Nashville • Camden • Kansas City

Library of Congress Cataloging in Publication Data

Davis, Ron Lee.
  Gold in the making.

  1. Presbyterian Church—Sermons. 2. Sermons, American.
I. Title.
BX9178.D37G64   1983   242'.4   83-21931
ISBN 0-8407-5869-3

11 12 - 97 96 95 94 93 92 91 90 89

Dedicated to our daughter Rachael
whose courageous battle against the last enemy motivated
me to write this book, and whose gentle life encourages
me to allow myself to be refined by God, that I might one
day come forth as gold.

"When He has tried me,
I shall come forth as gold."
Job 23:10 NASB

CONTENTS

FOREWORD

The best books, in Carlyle's words, "come flaming and burning out of the heart of a living man." The author's convictions and assertions must be shared. He or she is not so much writing a book to add to the literature of his or her time as witnessing to a personal experience. He or she wants everyone to share that experience and know with the same assurance what he or she has discovered.

This book on suffering is like that. It is not a compilation of the thoughts of others, or an arid discussion of philosophical theories. What we read was lived profoundly before it was written. There are few things more powerful than a gripping personal story, especially when it is told well. It engages the reader in living with the author what he has gone through and, with exclamation-point intensity, causes the reader to think about what it means to him or her.

Ron Davis is one of the most creative pastors in America. In this, his first book, we discover why. He has all the accouterments of a successful church leader. But more than his able mind, excellent training, and broad experience, he lives in depth. He has allowed God to speak to him personally in what he seeks to communicate. Out of his own suffering in the near death of his daughter and the precarious pregnancy of his wife with their second child, he allows his own heart to be pressed to the pulse-beat of the pathos, anxiety, unanswered questions, and excruciating tension of human suffering. This has put him in touch with the suffering of the people to whom he preaches and for whom he cares in the multiplicity of his pastoral work. Here is an example of a new breed of church leader. Devoid of professionalism and glib, pious phrases intoned with a stained-glass solemnity, Ron is a communicator of grace that has been experienced in the refining fires of in-depth living.

As I read this book, I felt as though Ron and I were engaged in a deep conversation about the meaning of the suffering we had both been through. His honesty about his own experience comes through in a way that constantly made me want to say, "I know what you mean. I've felt that too. Yes. I've ached over that question also, and yes, I've felt the same uneasiness when people have told me all I need is more faith or deeper confession." All through the book, whether asked in empathetical identification or implied by the writer's sensitivity, I heard, "You know what I mean, don't you?" And repeatedly as I read, my response was, "Yes, how did you know?" Only one who has really lived could know and write with such unencumbered directness coupled with tender love.

The author does more than identify. He has some bracing truths to share that are soundly biblical. They blow away the cobwebs of confused thinking. Pain, suffering, and trouble are a part of life. There's no escape. God does not send it, but He uses it to refine us into the great people He intended us to be. Suffering will make or break us. Here's a down-to-earth, penetrating book to help us get the best out of the problems we face. The author unwraps trouble, takes it apart, grapples with it, and helps us surrender it to God. But he doesn't stop there. He shows how the difficulties we go through enable us to be "wounded healers" toward people who also suffer. We learn how to share the suffering heart of the Lord.

A remarkable aspect of this book is its biblical clarity, illustrated by the real-life stories of people. Explanation of the truth never bogs down in complicated rhetoric. Each point is illustrated by the authentic experiences and discoveries of people who have been immersed in living beneath the surface of a placid, easy life. We are drawn into their lives, experience with them what they are going through, and learn with them what the Lord has allowed them to see.

Ron Davis is able to share these stories of real people because he has entered into their struggles as a caring friend and pastor. We are introduced to people who have earned the right through what they have suffered to tell us the secrets they have found and share them with unstudied honesty and humility.

This book will make you think, cry, and laugh. It will set you free from the panic of life's difficulties. You will be introduced to a man who has lived, hurt, and hoped, and with him you'll discover again, as I did, how to rejoice in the ups and downs of life. It will be difficult to put the book down once you start reading it, and when you're finished, you'll greet the future as a friend, knowing that what happens to you will be used by the Lord for what He wants to happen through you in the lives of others. Life's trials will be surrendered to the Refiner's fire and you will, like the author and the courageous people whose stories he tells, become gold in the making.

Lloyd John Ogilvie

ACKNOWLEDGMENTS

Perhaps you feel a sense of apprehension as you open this book. You may think, "What is God going to bring into my life if I allow Him to teach me about trials, grief, suffering, or death? Will He now bring some trial into my life, or the life of someone close to me? *I'm not sure I want to hear this!*"

I want you to know that you're not alone in asking these questions; I've wrestled with them myself. I believe it's understandable that we feel apprehension as we squarely face the facts about trials, suffering, and death. (Most of us, in fact, spend all our waking hours *not* facing these facts.) But I also believe that this feeling of apprehension is based on a *mis*apprehension of the love and faithfulness of God.

I want to encourage you. I want you to know that God loves you totally, absolutely, and unconditionally. He loves you better and more completely than you love yourself. He wants to heal you, not hurt you. He wants to mend your brokenness and make you whole. He desires what is best for you as you seek to be conformed into the image of His Son, and He has given you promises of His peace. These promises are reliable and dependable; He's given you His Word on that.

I invite you to join with me—confidently trusting in God's everlasting, fatherly love for your life—as I relate my pilgrimage of coming to see more clearly His plan and purpose for the trials that inevitably touch us all.

As we begin, I'd like to acknowledge the help and encouragement I've received from others during the writing of this book.

I have found in Jim Denney not only a sensitive and discerning writer, but a dear and special brother in Christ. His questions, observations, and editing of my material have given to this book what I alone never could have hoped to achieve.

Much of the material in this book has been presented to my family of faith at First Presbyterian Church in Fresno, California, and I'm grateful for them and for their suggestions. Tess Mott, Linda Osborne, Doug Armey, Bobbye Temple, and Debbie Denney have all participated in editing this manuscript, and I'm deeply thankful for them.

Thanks also to Dr. Brent Lindquist, Executive Director of Link Care Center, Fresno, California, and to Dr. Tom Granata, who contributed their caring and insightful observations as professional Christian psychologists.

I must express my deep gratitude to my editor at Thomas Nelson Publishers, Peter Gillquist. Long before I believed enough in myself to consider writing a book, Peter encouraged me, and he stood by me through the entire editorial process.

Special appreciation must go to my wife, Shirley, who carefully critiqued each chapter, and whose suggestions and encouragement have been so important to the shaping of this book.

Most of all, I'm deeply grateful to the scores of friends who have been courageous and open enough to permit me to share the stories of their trials with you. Their honesty and vulnerability for the sake of others and the kingdom of God have taught me many of the lessons and truths that I discuss in these pages.

1. OH, NO, NOT THIS!

A Practical, Biblical Definition of Suffering

In this you greatly rejoice, though now for a little while, if need be, you have been grieved by various trials, that the genuineness of your faith, being much more precious than gold that perishes, though it is tested by fire, may be found to praise, honor, and glory at the revelation of Jesus Christ (1 Pet. 1:6–7).

Our daughter Rachael was born eleven weeks prematurely. She weighed only three pounds at birth and within a few days her weight dropped even further.

Soon Rachael's breathing became labored. The doctors determined that, as a consequence of being born almost three months prematurely, she had contracted hyaline membrane disease, a serious respiratory distress. Shortly this infection was complicated by several additional lung infections. From the hospital where she was born, she was rushed by ambulance to Children's Hospital in downtown Minneapolis. There she was kept in an incubator for the first six weeks of her life. Each day was a life-struggle for Rachael, but she gradually gained weight and strength. Finally she was allowed to come home.

Within four months, the joy of that moment once more turned to anxiety. At 3:00 A.M. on a Sunday, Rachael was again rushed to Children's Hospital. The diagnosis was pneumonia, with other pulmonary complications. Our infant was kept alive by a respirator (which did all of her breathing for her) and a drug that temporarily paralyzed her whole body.

Scores of Christians from around the country joined in prayer for Rachael's life, and within three weeks she again returned home—but with orders from the physician that she be kept in total isolation for the first year of her life. Our pediatric radiologist later told us that he never had seen or read of a baby born so prematurely, with so many lung infections, who had lived.

So began a year of trial for my wife, Shirley, and me. Rachael required feedings every two hours, twenty-four hours a day. Under such a ceaseless day-and-night schedule of feedings and changings, coupled with our concern that she might become sick again, we became tense, emotionally frayed, physically exhausted. Shirley and I began to discover fragile, brittle places in our own personalities, in our faith, and in our relationship together. We were frustrated at being unable to share our new baby with our friends and family. We were forced to share Rachael's isolation (or imprisonment, as it often seemed) in our house.

It was a difficult year for our marriage, and for my work as a pastor. Even though we loved that baby dearly, and even though we would have gladly suffered any amount of strain and deprivation for the sake of that precious little girl—that year was a time of real trial and difficulty for our family.

But through that time of testing—when Rachael was most critically ill and when things seemed the most bleak—Shirley and I discovered in brand-new ways how God cares for His children; how His love touches us through the lives of other believers; how God's strength is perfected in our frailness and weakness; how God can transform our affliction into witness and ministry for His glory and the good of others; and most of all, how times of trial and suffering serve to refine the precious metal of Christian character.

Today Rachael is alive and healthy, and her life teaches us new things daily about the love and caring of God, our Father. Had we not gone through this period of anxiety and stress during Rachael's first year, I believe Shirley and I would be very different people today than we are—perhaps with less first-hand knowledge of God's care, and less capacity to trust His perfect will. Certainly we have far to go, but we can already see how our trials have begun the job of chipping and sanding and smoothing the rough edges from our Christian character.

Call it grief, suffering, or affliction. By whatever name, it is inevitable that trial will come into your life and mine. Many promises in the Scriptures are precious to us, but one we would rather not hear was given to us by Jesus Christ Himself: "In the world you will have tribulation" (John 16:33). If we want to speak the truth, if we want to be true to the witness of the Scriptures, we have to acknowledge that the Christian life is not an unending mountaintop experience; the Christian life is filled with deep valleys.

Oh, No, Not This!

When we hear the words *trial* or *suffering*, we often associate them with disease, pain, an accidental injury, or some other kind of physical trauma—and this is indeed the sort of trial we are sometimes called upon to face. But I'd like to define these words in a much broader sense: *Suffering is anything that makes us think, "Oh, no, not this!"*

It may be cancer or a sore throat. It may be the illness or loss of someone close to you. It may be a personal failure or disappointment in your job or school work. It may be a rumor that is circulating in your office or your church, damaging your reputation, bringing you grief and anxiety. It might be a broken relationship with a family member or a friend. It's painful, and it wounds you deeply. It's suffering.

I grew up surrounded by a loving family and close friends, and I enjoyed a happy life in a small community. In fact, I believe that God in His grace kept me in a cocoon of comfort and safety for the first twenty-five years of my life. But you can't build character in a cocoon. It's warm and safe and un-threatening there, but you don't become like Christ in a co-coon. In His timing, God—again, in His all-sufficient grace —removed me from that cocoon; at the age of twenty-five, my life suddenly changed.

First, my father—a Presbyterian minister who had always enjoyed excellent health—was suddenly stricken with a heart attack in our home town in Iowa. This beloved man, my dearest friend, passed away at age sixty-five.

Just two months later, my mother was discovered to have a tumor; in surgery, the doctors discovered a trace of malig-nancy. More anxiety, more questioning, more trial, but in this case the Lord brought complete healing.

Then there was the birth of Rachael—an event of mingled joy and anxiety, followed by a year of isolation and testing. Three years later, Shirley was forced to spend the last half of her second pregnancy completely bedridden, due to a condi-tion called an "incompetent cervix," as we awaited the birth of our son Nathan.

My trials may seem small or great, compared with what you have undergone in your life or what you are going through right now. Our troubles come in different packages. But they hurt, don't they? They really hurt.

The Process of Suffering

Suffering is mysterious. Suffering is more than a personal problem, a personal trial; it's a staggering theological problem, a deep mystery of God. We ask, "Why does a loving, omnipotent God allow suffering?" Or, "Why do trial and illness and grief and death come into our lives seemingly at random, without apparent meaning, striking the good as well as the wicked, the great as well as the weak and powerless?" And often we ask, "Why me?"

Your troubles are not meaningless, random events that crash into your life without purpose or pattern. Biblically, suffering is part of a *process*: "We know that suffering produces perseverance; perseverance, character; and character, hope" (Rom. 5:3–4 NIV). We all want the product, character; but we don't want the process, suffering.

David was a gifted young pastor, a graduate of Denver Seminary. People said David had the potential of being one of the leading evangelical pastors in America. He had a true love for the people in his church; a true gift of making the gospel clear and real and compelling to his listeners; and a heart that was true and obedient to his Lord. David was not only a big man spiritually, he was a big man physically: he stood well over six feet tall, and weighed about two hundred pounds.

At the age of thirty-two, David was found to have cancer—an advanced case that had metastasized throughout his body. The disease quickly took its toll on him, and his weight dropped from about two hundred pounds to just sixty pounds.

A few days before David went from this life into eternity, his father—a man who loves Jesus Christ—visited David in his hospital room. They talked for a while, each seeking words to console the other in the shadow of imminent death and loss.

Then David said, "Dad, do you remember when I was a little boy and you used to pick me up and hold me in your arms?" In reply, his father knelt down and picked up his sixty-pound, thirty-two-year-old son and hugged him—just hugged him, not a word spoken.

David looked up at his father and said, "Dad, thanks. Thank you for building into my life the faith in Jesus Christ that enables me to face even a moment like this."

We all want faith like that, we all want character, but we don't want suffering. We all want the product, but we don't want the process.

Before our family moved to the West Coast, I had the privilege for six years of serving as Bible teacher for the Minnesota Vikings. During that time I came to know Karl Kassulke, the Vikings' starting cornerback in the mid-1970s. Karl was not a Christian when I first met him. He was a very successful, very self-sufficient professional football player. One day Karl's self-sufficiency came to a sudden halt when he was severely injured in a motorcycle accident, which left him totally paralyzed from the neck down.

That accident began a process in Karl's life that led to a new, meaningful, personal encounter with Jesus Christ. God is using Karl's paralysis, his insufficiency, to teach him about His *all*-sufficiency. As Karl describes in his recent book, *Kassulke*, God is building in him Christlike character and a vital relationship with Himself:

> Obviously, I didn't think I needed that motorcycle accident. But that was what it took to bring me to my knees. I don't think I ever would have done it otherwise. It was what I needed. It was God's grace to me.

You may not be suffering from a paralyzing injury like Karl's, or from the prospect of imminent death as Dave did, or from a problem pregnancy like Shirley's. But if you're a Christian, you will be tried. It's a promise from God.

No "Ten Easy Steps"

You may be going through a painful trial right now. Perhaps that trial has lasted longer than you ever dreamed it would; your way is not clear, and you're beginning to wonder if it will ever end. Or perhaps your time of greatest trial is still ahead. Whatever your situation, I believe (and pray) that these words have come to you for a purpose— as a source of encouragement for you, or as a source of strength that you can draw on and share with another who is undergoing trial right now.

This book is no lofty theological treatise on the problem of suffering, nor any kind of an "answer book," nor a "ten-easy-steps-to-conquer-suffering" kind of book. There are no pat answers to the trials we face. My passionate hope is that these words be practical, biblical, helpful, and hopeful. My prayer is that this book will be used by God to help build your faith, and to bring you strength and encouragement.

I'm certainly not sharing with you from a sense of having mastered sorrow and pain. Any exhortation or any word of comfort I give you I must first direct to myself, because I'm just like you—a fellow struggler, a sojourner with you, frail and prone to disease, loss, death, and sin.

But I'm bold enough to believe that where there is affliction and trial and suffering in the lives of believers, there is a beautiful process of purification taking place: the precious metal of Christian character is being refined for God's use. There is *gold in the making*—gold for the church of Jesus Christ, gold for the kingdom of God, gold for your life and for your eternity with Jesus.

2. *WHEN HE HAS TRIED ME*

Five Principles—and a Promise

But He knows the way I take; when He has tried me, I shall come forth as gold (Job 23:10 NASB).

When Shirley became pregnant for the second time, our doctor had us take certain precautions to prevent another premature delivery. The cause of Rachael's premature birth, he said, was an "incompetent cervix," a weakened opening at the base of the womb. The enemy was gravity; the cervix was not strong enough to ensure that the fetus would be held in place. On the doctor's advice, we limited Shirley's activity, and she had checkups on a weekly basis. Of course, we prayed.

But one night, at the beginning of the second trimester of her pregnancy, Shirley began to experience severe abdominal pain. We rushed her to the hospital, where the doctors told us she would miscarry without an operation to repair her cervix. The surgeons quickly performed the operation, a procedure that would not entirely correct the problem, but would keep it in check for the time being. The doctors ordered that for the remainder of her pregnancy, for the next four months, Shirley should be totally confined in bed, lying on her back.

The day after surgery, two of our friends came to visit Shirley in her hospital room. "Shirley," they said, "we want you to know that we've been praying for you. We've claimed a miracle of healing for you. You can disregard what your physicians said about lying on your back for the next four months. In fact, you can get up from your hospital bed and begin walking right now. The Lord has healed you."

Shirley disregarded their counsel. She stayed on her back in bed for four months. At the end of that time our son Nathan was born right on schedule, nine pounds eight ounces, completely healthy, and with no complications.

Perhaps you've had a similar experience during an injury or illness, when someone has given you similar counsel. "Miraculous healing is the only solution to your sickness. There's no other option," someone may have told you. "Sickness is never the will of God. The devil is at work in your sickness, and God will wait until you can muster up enough faith to be healed."

Or perhaps someone has come to you in your time of trial and said, "What you need is to reflect on what God is trying to teach you through all this. Surely your life has become displeasing to God in some way. Is there some unconfessed sin in your life? You must have stepped outside of God's will, and He's just waiting for you to turn back to Him so He can heal you."

You may have been visited in your time of suffering by a self-appointed spiritual cheerleader, the kind of relentless optimist who brings flowers, sings songs, small-talks through the entire visit—and immediately switches the subject if you turn to talk about your illness or trial. This person's solution to suffering is to deny suffering, to blithely, cheerily ignore suffering; maybe it'll go away.

Or you may have been visited in your trial by someone who tells you that the answer to your problem is praise—not just praise in the midst of suffering, but praise because of the suffering. They'll tell you, "You need to be able to say, 'God, I love You for letting me suffer like this. Praise the Lord, I've got cancer!' or 'Praise the Lord, I've lost my job!' or 'Praise the Lord, I've lost my dearest loved one.' "

I've known many instances where this kind of advice has been given to a suffering or grieving or depressed person by good, well-intentioned Christians. Such people are usually trying to help, trying to offer a word of encouragement, trying to console. But if you've ever been on the receiving end of such consolation, you know how it is often the last thing you need to hear in a difficult time. Such words often add to your pain, compound your trial with a sense of guilt, and confuse you in your search for God's meaning and strength for the present trial.

Worst of all, every one of these responses to suffering is, by itself, unbiblical. Miraculous healing is not God's only means of healing. Suffering does not occur only as a consequence of unconfessed sin or God's displeasure. Suffering cannot be treated by denial and jolly good cheer. And while the Bible tells us to rejoice in the midst of our trials, God does not always expect us to rejoice because of our suffering (though, by the grace of God, even that is often possible).

When we encounter trial or suffering, we need to cling to the simple promise that Christ is there with us, suffering with us; that He is "a Man of Sorrows, acquainted with grief." We must keep our eyes focused on Jesus, even though they are filled with tears. Most of all, we need to be aware of what the Bible promises—and what it does not promise—about the trials and struggles of this life.

If you've ever been confused by some of the well-meaning but unbiblical counsel on suffering, the distorted voices that we hear so often today, then let me suggest another view, a more encouraging and, I think, a more biblical view of God's plan for life's hard places.

I want to begin by showing you five principles that form the basis of a biblical understanding of suffering.

Principle Number One

Most human suffering can be partially comprehended when we understand a biblical definition of free will. This principle is implicit throughout the Scriptures. In Romans 1:18–32, for example, Paul gave a specific, categoric description of the ravaging effects of human rebellion against God through the free will God has given human beings. It is rebellion against God (both Adam's and ours, as members of Adam's race) that has brought most of the suffering and pain into this world, into our own lives, and into the lives of others around us.

During the time I was preparing a series of messages on suffering, my friend Keith Phillips (director of World Impact, a ministry of lifestyle evangelism to the inner cities) told me about a young man who had come to Christ, had been freed from bondage to drug abuse, and was growing in his faith and Christian maturity. Just as he was preparing to assume a responsible role in the work of World Impact, he was tragically, senselessly murdered by a gang member, one of his old acquaintances.

Like that gang member, we are all given free will by God's sovereignty. We choose in our free will to be in rebellion against God, and that rebellion brings pain, suffering, and grief to those around us.

Principle Number Two

Because of human rebellion, all creation has been marred; we live in a fallen world. The beauty that remains in this world is leftover beauty from Creation, before the Fall. In this world, Satan is the "prince of the power of the air" (see Eph. 2:2). Satan seeks to bring havoc, suffering, and pain to any of us in any way he can. Satan may be the prince of this world, but Jesus Christ is the Lord of the universe.

Several years ago, Joni Eareckson Tada and her sister Cathy were swimming off Chesapeake Bay. Joni dived into shallow water, struck a rock, and was paralyzed from the neck down. In her book *Joni*, she writes:

> I believe that Satan wanted to ruin my life, the life of a 17-year-old girl. He wanted to break my neck and put me into a hospital for a couple of years and hinder my faith in God. He wanted to destroy my family. It was Satan-sponsored confusion and heartbreak that steeped me deeper and deeper into bitterness. But God has a miraculous way of reaching down into our suffering and wrenching a real and positive good for Him out of it all.

Living victoriously even in the grip of a paralyzing affliction, Joni is a witness to the power of God to accomplish His purpose in a fallen world. The Bible tells us that Satan is the prince of this world (see 2 Cor. 4:4; Eph. 2:1-2; 6:12), but Jesus is the King over all.

Principle Number Three

Our suffering is always shared by Christ. "Surely He has borne our griefs/And carried our sorrows...," says Isaiah 53:4. What a great consolation to us! Whatever you are suffering today—loneliness, alienation or separation from your spouse, child, or parent, disease or injury, an unwanted pregnancy, the loss of your home or your job, or just the process of growing older and the fear of that great enemy, death—God Himself, in the Person of Jesus Christ, has borne that very suffering on Calvary's cross.

One of my favorite promises of Scripture is this: "I am with you." In fact, I'm more and more convinced that this simple promise from the Father is the central, the most consistent, the most common promise in the entire Bible. It is perhaps most familiar to us in Psalm 23:4: "Yea, though I walk through the valley of the shadow of death,/I will fear no evil;/For *You are with me* . . ." (italics mine).

Many times pastors, evangelists, and lay Christians, in their zeal to win others to Christ, have painted a picture of the Christian life that doesn't exist: a life of success, of health and prosperity, of one delightful experience after another. I've never found a Scripture verse that says the Christian life is a life of ease. Accordingly, I believe that "selling" Christianity in such a way robs Scripture of its integrity and cheats the prospective convert of the truth. Selling a prospective convert to Christianity on an illusion will only lead to disillusion when he finds out for himself the truth about the Christian life.

And what is the truth about the Christian life? The truth is that true obedience and allegiance to the lordship of our Savior Jesus Christ demands sacrifice, it demands a change in lifestyle from that of the world's culture to that of the Kingdom. Conversion to Christ is not the point at which all problems cease; it is in a very real sense the place where one's real challenges and heartbreaks begin. The Christian life is often one of valleys and deep pits and dark shadows of discouragement, loneliness, and betrayal. You may be experiencing this reality of the Christian life right now. But praise God for His promise: "Thou art with me." Christ is right here with us, sharing in our suffering.

Principle Number Four

God wants to take our suffering and transform it into witness for Him. This principle is vividly demonstrated in the lives of people like Joni Eareckson and Karl Kassulke. But let me offer another example.

Kim Kostron is a special friend of ours from Minneapolis; she often babysat for us when we lived in the Twin Cities area. Kim was the number one ranked speed skater in the world at her distance. For four years she trained hard and singlemindedly for one goal, one dream, one objective: the Olympic Games. She was seeded number one in the trials and we all pulled for her as we watched on television. On the day of her trials, Kim didn't skate quite as fast as usual; she finished fourth—by four hundredths of a second. The first three skaters would race in the Olympics, while the fourth would serve as an alternate. Four years of preparation to race in the Olympics—and she had not made it.

But Jesus Christ was with Kim in her disappointment. On the same day that she placed fourth in the Olympic time trials, Kim was in the locker room, seated by a lady who had watched her skate. "Kim," said the woman, watching Kim's calm composure, "how are you able to handle the disappointment?"

"Well, it's because I've given my life to Christ," Kim replied, "and He gives me strength." Not that Kim was bubbling with joy in the midst of her defeat—far from it. But she was experiencing in the depth of her disappointment the peace that passes understanding. To paraphrase the apostle Paul in 2 Corinthians 4:8–9, we are often discouraged but we are never in despair, often knocked down but never knocked out, surrounded by enemies but never without a Friend.

That day, the woman sitting next to Kim in that locker room gave her life to Christ. Today she serves Christ in a mighty way because Kim Kostron was willing to let her time of trial and disappointment be transformed into witness for Christ.

As I was writing this book, our congregation in Fresno was praying for a beautiful, winsome fourteen-year-old Christian girl in her courageous battle against leukemia. Stacy Nantz has just passed from this life into eternity.

Stacy was a very special young lady. She never let the fact that she was young or that she was suffering from a fatal disease keep her from sharing her faith in Jesus Christ with others. On the occasions that I visited Stacy in her hospital room, I often came away cheered, touched, and blessed by her beautiful spirit.

During the final weeks of Stacy's life, my young friend met a fifteen-year-old girl I'll call Maria. Maria, also, was terminally ill and being cared for on the same ward of the hospital with Stacy. She had literally grown up on the streets. Throughout her life, she had known abuse and loneliness. She'd had a baby at the age of thirteen. She was bitter and hostile toward everyone she met, and a stream of curses poured continually from her mouth. One time she had scratched a doctor's face as he bent down to check her, and another time her fists had rained blows on a nurse who was trying to care for her.

Then Stacy came into Maria's life.

As a result of Stacy's patient, loving, courageous witness for Jesus Christ in the face of suffering and death, that lonely and broken young girl gave her life to the Lord. There was a marvelous change in Maria's attitude. Her doctors, nurses, and family were amazed to notice the attitude of thankfulness and love that had grown in her life. Where once there was cursing and hatred, there now was praise and the peace of God, passing everyone's understanding.

Maria preceded Stacy by a few days into the presence of the Lord. Today, Stacy Nantz and her new sister in Christ are together in the presence of God—all because one fourteen-year-old girl was willing to take her suffering and allow it to be transformed into witness for Jesus Christ, even in the final days of her life.

Principle Number Five

When there has been extreme pain, there often must be significant time for healing. Unfortunately, we have not allowed much room for the time element in our theology. Instead, our treatment for a deep emotional wound is "instant healing." We give people "six easy steps to overcome trials." We tell hurting people to claim victory over their struggles.

If you've ever struggled with severe depression, or if you've ever grieved and suffered because a friend you loved and trusted has broken your heart, or if you've ever struggled with anger and bitterness because your employer has passed you over for advancement, or if you've become weary in well-doing in your Christian ministry, I want to give you a word of encouragement. Perhaps the terrible circumstances of your trial have ended, but you're still left wondering when the pain of it—the anger or the sorrow of it—will end. You've possibly received counsel from well-meaning Christian friends. You don't need to hear any more sermons right now.

You just need some *time.*

The people I know who are the most spiritually, emotionally, and physically healthy are the ones who know that when there has been a time of extreme trial or pain or injury, there also needs to be an extended time of healing. At the end of that time, they will come forth with a perspective on suffering that is God's own perspective.

It's the mother who, after a time of healing, is able to say to God in the midst of an incredible loss, "You gave, You have now taken away. Blessed be the name of the Lord."

It's the father who has lost his job but, after a time of healing, is able to say to his wife and children, "Let's get together tonight and thank God for this opportunity to trust Him and see what new adventure He's giving us as a family."

It's the high school student who has gone through the pain of rejection by his or her peers but, after a time of healing, is able to say, "I'll stand up for my principles anyway. I'll maintain my standards even though I feel like I'm all alone at school, because I know I'm not alone. God is with me."

If you have a friend or a family member who is going through a time of great darkness and trial in his or her life, I want to encourage you not to charge into that person's life with a lot of advice or cheery clichés. Rather, step back. Often the way you can help most is to get off that person's back. Be available. Pray for the person in the privacy of your own devotion to God. Give the one you love time to heal.

And Now The Promise

Let me close this chapter with a promise. In my own life, the promises I treasure most, next to the promises of our salvation in Christ, are those that tell us that in the midst of our suffering and trial, it's worth it all.

Of these, my favorite is found in the Old Testament in the book of Job. In the course of this journal of affliction, Job had lost his land, his health, and his ten children. Finally he cried out, his soul struggling under the weight of his misery: "Oh, that I knew where I might find Him!. . . I go forward, but He is not there, And backward, but I cannot perceive Him . . ." (Job 23:3,8).

Have you ever felt like that? It's okay to feel like that! Job cried out, "Where are you, God?" If you feel that way, go to God with your true feelings and say it. Don't ever let anyone make you feel "unspiritual" because you feel, along with Job,

"Oh, that I knew where I might find Him!"

Now the promise (Job 23:10 NASB): "But He knows the way I take; *When He has tried me, I shall come forth as gold*" (italics mine). Notice that the key to this promise is "when He has tested me."

You see, there's no such thing as "instant gold refining." The process of refining and purifying and perfecting gold takes time and it takes a great deal of heat. But look at the result! Something lasting, something of beauty, something of value. *Gold.* Christian character is a precious metal that, like gold, is refined by time and the fiery trials of life into something eternal, something beautiful and valuable for the Master.

Affliction is gold in the making for the child of God, and God is the one who holds the timepiece. If you don't remember anything else I say here, please note this: *for the Christian, affliction is gold in the making.* If we will cooperate in the process, we will come forth as gold.

Why cooperate with God in being refined? Why continue to stand against the strong current of loss, heartache, stress, and pain? Because it is in the hot forge of trials that true Christian character is shaped, hammered, tempered, and matured. It's there that the life of Jesus Christ is given its maximum opportunity to become part of our very own life. It's there that our thin, fragile veneer of theology is replaced by a tough, reliable hide of convictions that enable us to face and handle life instead of escaping from it.

God understands the heartache you feel, brought about by the evil that He mysteriously permits. He understands because Jesus Christ, the Man of Sorrows, has taken all our pain onto Himself, and thus into the very heart of God Himself. He understands. He wants to bring you into such a tender relationship with Himself that you will one day be able to stand with Job and say with unshakable conviction, "He knows the way I take, and when He has tried me, I shall come forth as gold."

3. A STRATEGY FOR SUFFERING

What Does It Mean to "Rejoice in our Sufferings"?

We also rejoice in our sufferings, because we know that suffering produces perseverance; perseverance, character; and character, hope. And hope does not disappoint us, because God has poured out his love into our hearts by the Holy Spirit, whom he has given us (Rom. 5:3–5 NIV).

A girl and her father were out for their customary morning walk at a golf course near their home. The girl was walking just a few steps in front of the father, though *walking* is probably not the right word. Actually she lurched along, clumsily, unsteadily. She was severely handicapped, severely retarded, severely deformed. This girl and her father had taken this walk on many other mornings like this, but there was one difference on this day: the father carried a revolver. The man and his daughter walked over the green hillside and down into a dell. First one shot rang out, and then a second, echoing across that placid golf course and into the village. A few moments later the bodies of both father and daughter were found side by side, sprawled in the grass. The people in that family and in the community asked the question, "Why does a God of love allow such suffering?"

A woman I know poured her entire life into her husband and children. Over the years, her children grew up and moved far away, and one day her husband died. Alone and widowed, she spent her days watching television. She had no friends. She suffered from an abysmal loneliness, and it was out of that loneliness she came to me, her pastor. "Why does God allow me, near the end of my life, to suffer so much?" she asked.

Tears streamed down my face as I performed the baptismal service, not in a church sanctuary but in a hospital room. I performed it for little Steven, a baby only seven months old. Steven had been critically ill from the day he was born. I stood with his parents and together we shared in the rites of baptism. A few weeks later I was to participate in Steven's funeral service.

There is one promise of Scripture that we dare not forget if we are to be honest with ourselves and with God. It's this simple promise of Jesus Christ, found in John 16:33: "In the world you will have tribulation. . . ." This is a difficult promise. We don't want to think about tribulation, especially when we are comfortable and at ease. But this is the witness of Jesus Christ and the Bible.

Paul declared, "We must through many tribulations enter the kingdom of God" (Acts 14:22). Peter wrote, "Beloved, do not think it strange concerning the fiery trial which is to try you...but rejoice . . ." (1 Pet. 4:12–13). And James wrote, "My brethren, count it all joy when you fall into various trials, knowing that the testing of your faith produces patience" (James 1:2–3).

Suffering is inevitable! So what is our response? Should we pity ourselves in our suffering? Should we dread the future and try to hide from the sufferings and trials it holds? The apostle Paul said *no!* Rather, "we also rejoice in our sufferings, because we know that suffering produces perseverance; perseverance, character; and character, hope" (Rom. 5:3 NIV). Rejoice in suffering? That's right.

But understand this: when Paul said, "rejoice in suffering," he clearly did not suggest masochism—that we should "enjoy" suffering. Nor did Paul advocate Stoicism, where we become indifferent and fatalistic about suffering. Nor did he propose a kind of sentimentalism that pretends there is no suffering. Rejoicing is a practical, livable, biblical strategy for responding to the trials that will surely come our way. The same Scriptures that promise us suffering also give us a powerful strategy for attaining the victory over suffering, for rejoicing in the midst of it.

Let's break that strategy down into four parts.

Strategy for Suffering Number One: Identify with Christ

We can rejoice in the midst of suffering because we know that it brings us identification with Jesus Christ. Jesus identified with us when He became like us, suffered, and died for us. "We see Jesus, who was made a little lower than the angels, for the suffering of death crowned with glory and honor, that He, by the grace of God, might taste death for everyone. . . . In that He Himself has suffered, being tempted, He is able to aid those who are tempted" (Heb. 2:9,18; see also Phil. 2:5–8; Heb. 4:14–16).

In return we have the privilege to identify with Christ through our sufferings. "Beloved," wrote Peter, "do not think it strange concerning the fiery trial which is to try you, as though some strange thing happened to you; but *rejoice to the extent that you partake of Christ's sufferings*, that when His glory is revealed, you may also be glad with exceeding joy" (1 Pet. 4:12–13, italics mine). This is an encouraging affirmation of the coming glory, beyond the present trials, by a man who knew Christ, and who knew suffering.

When we suffer, we have an opportunity to identify with Christ and His sufferings to a depth that we can experience at no other time and in no other way in all of life. "I want to know Christ," wrote the apostle Paul, "and the power of his resurrection *and the fellowship of sharing in his sufferings, becoming like him in his death,* and so, somehow, to attain to the resurrection from the dead" (Phil. 3:10 NIV, italics mine).

If the goal of our lives as Christians is to know Christ and become like Him, then ultimately we must welcome anything that will enable that process to take place. One ingredient in the process of becoming conformed to the image of Christ, according to the Scriptures, is participation with Jesus in His suffering. As that process progresses, as we become more and more like Him, we'll find ourselves able to say with Paul, "The sufferings of this present time are not worthy to be compared with the glory which shall be revealed in us" (Rom. 8:18).

In the difficult times of my own life, I often return to the words of Isaiah 53:4: "Surely He has borne our griefs, and carried our sorrows. . . ." Whatever your grief, whatever your sorrow—whether a sore throat or cancer—you can be comforted in knowing that Jesus Christ has borne that very grief on the cross; He has borne that very sorrow and carried it for you.

At the beginning of Romans 5 Paul wrote that, as a result of Christ's sacrificial suffering on the cross, "we have peace with God." Now, this is not the peace *of* God that Paul spoke about in Philippians or Galatians, where he was talking about the fruit of the Spirit. In Romans 5, Paul used a different preposition; he was talking about peace *with* God. Whether or not you feel peace in your heart, the fact is that the strife is now over. There is peace with God; we are reconciled with the Father. "We have peace with God through our Lord Jesus Christ" (Rom. 5:1).

What we begin to realize as we grow in our faith in Christ is that Christ did not come and die that we might not suffer, but that our suffering might be like His. Jesus Christ, the one who has borne our griefs all the way to the cross, says to us, "You don't have to suffer loneliness anymore—you have a friend. You don't have to be afraid anymore—you have a comforter."

What was Christ's suffering like? It was sacrificial. It was redemptive. It was suffering that was experienced as He poured His life out, not for Himself, but for others. He was wounded for our transgressions.

I confess that one of the tragic things in my life is that much of my suffering has not been patterned after that of Christ's. Much of my suffering has resulted because I have been sensitive to criticism and easily hurt. Directed inward, this sensitivity becomes an open wound in my own personality, a psychological and spiritual disability producing a particularly unChristlike suffering in my life.

Sensitivity is not in itself a flaw; in reality it's a God-given trait. Directed outward, it becomes a force to serve and love others in Christ's name. My most fervent prayer before the Father is frequently, "God, please take the sensitivity that You've given me and transform it. Channel it, so that my sensitivity can go out to the lonely, the forgotten, and the broken. Lord, make me sensitive for others and not for myself, and conform my character and my suffering to Yours."

Strategy for Suffering Number Two: Allow Suffering to Produce Character

We can rejoice in the midst of our suffering, knowing that suffering produces character. The more Paul suffered and endured, the stronger his character became. Finally, after having seen the hand of God uphold him through the trials of his life, he knew he could trust the hand of God even through the trials of a martyr's death. And who of us, when we face that last great enemy, death itself, does not want to face it with that assurance, faith, and strength of character?

Tom Landry, head coach of the Dallas Cowboys football team, explains his philosophy of coaching this way: "My task as a coach is to renew the minds of my players [which reminds us of Romans 12:1–2] and to get them to do things they do not want to do in order to achieve what they want to achieve." That's my task as a parent and a pastor, and I think that's the task of each of us as fellow strugglers and fellow followers of Jesus Christ. Let's encourage each other to do the things we do not want to do in order to achieve what we want to achieve.

We all want to achieve character, yet none of us wants to go through suffering. But suffering produces character.

In *The Problem of Pain* C. S. Lewis called suffering "God's megaphone." He wrote, "God whispers to us in our pleasures, speaks in our conscience, but God shouts in our pains." Suffering has a way of getting our attention, doesn't it? Suffering causes us to listen to God in a way nothing else in life can.

I recently had a conversation with a young man who made no claim to being a Christian. He said, "One thing that bothers me about Christianity is all these people I know, or who I've heard of, who've become Christians because of some suffering, some injury that ended their career in sports, or the death of some close friend. I just don't like a God who won't pay attention to us until we suffer. I just can't accept a God like that."

"You know," I said, "it's not a question of God paying attention to us. It's a question of our paying attention to Him."

He considered that for a moment, then said, "Well, that's true. But I still can't accept a God who lets us wait until suffering comes before He reaches to us or we turn to Him."

"Then why wait?" I said. "Why not turn to Him now?"

This young man had put his finger on the logical conclusion of his own objections: Shouldn't we listen to God now as He whispers to us, so that He doesn't have to shout to us later? The answer seemed self-evident, but he was unwilling to accept it. We are all often like this young man.

Call it self-sufficiency, call it perversity, call it the blindness of sin. It's a sad fact of our human nature that when things are going well, God seems to have an especially hard time gaining our attention. And it is at those times that God has to "shout" to get us to notice. C. S. Lewis went on to say,

> God knows what we are and that our happiness lies in Him. Yet we will not seek it in Him as long as He leaves us any other resort where it can be looked for. While what we call "our own life" remains agreeable, we will not surrender it to Him. What then can God do in our interest but make "our own life" less agreeable to us and take away the sources of our false happiness? It is just here, where God's providence seems at first to be most cruel that He deserves our greatest praise (from *The Problem of Pain*).

Christ comes to us in our suffering not because He prefers to, but because it is often only at such times that we will accept Him.

When we are faced with painful circumstances that we cannot change, we must—by faith—allow those circumstances to change us. That is the biblical response to suffering, the response that produces character. Job, as we saw earlier, understood this principle well.

That tried veteran, the apostle Paul, also understood this principle. Near the end of his life he was able to write, "We are hard pressed on every side, yet not crushed; we are perplexed, but not in despair; persecuted, but not forsaken; struck down, but not destroyed" (2 Cor. 4:8–9).

The person of tried Christian character, having stood all

through suffering, can still stand. Suffering produces character.

Strategy for Suffering Number Three: Choose your Attitude

We can rejoice in our sufferings as we learn to choose our own attitudes. "Let this mind be in you which was also in Christ Jesus," wrote Paul in Philippians 2:5. In other words, we can choose the attitude we will have. The attitude we should choose is that of Jesus Christ. And what was the attitude of Jesus? Philippians 2:6–8 tells us that He humbled Himself, took the form of a servant, and obediently submitted to His circumstances—the death of the cross.

St. John Chrysostom was one of the fathers of the Christian church in the fourth century A.D. Because he boldly proclaimed that Jesus, not the Roman Caesar, was Lord, Chrysostom was arrested and tried before the Roman emperor Arcaduis. As Arcaduis pondered the punishment he should mete out to Chrysostom, he first threatened him with banishment.

"But, sir," replied Chrysostom, "it's impossible for you to banish me from my home, because the whole world is my Father's house."

Arcaduis then threatened to confiscate all his possessions. But Chrysostom replied, "My treasures are in heaven, where no one can break through and steal."

The emperor then said, "I will cast you into prison, and shut you away not only from your friends but from all human contact." Chrysostom replied, "I have a Friend who has promised never to leave me or forsake me."

Exasperated, Arcaduis angrily threatened him with death. But Chrysostom replied, "Death has no terror for me. My life is hidden with Christ."

What could the emperor do with Chrysostom? He was truly free, regardless of his circumstances—free from slavery, imprisonment, and the fear of death. Like Chrysostom, we as Christians can choose to have the attitude of Jesus Christ within us.

I firmly believe that circumstances compose only 10 percent of life; the other 90 percent is attitude. If we choose an attitude of gratitude in every area of life, we can control our response to life. We don't have to be controlled by our circumstances.

Victor Frankl, the eminent German Jewish doctor, was arrested by the Gestapo during World War II. As he was being interrogated by the Nazi secret police, he was stripped of all his possessions—his clothes, his jewelry, his wedding band. He was imprisoned for days without knowing whether his family was alive or dead. His head was shaved. He was repeatedly taken from his prison cell and forced to stand naked under bright lights through grueling periods of questioning. He underwent many savage, senseless tortures.

He later said that, stripped of everything, he realized he had only one thing left:

> I realized I still had the power to choose my own attitude. No matter what happened now, the attitude choice was mine to make. Bitterness or forgiveness, to give up or to go on, hatred or hope—the attitude was still mine and no one in the Gestapo could take away my attitude (quoted by Dale E. Galloway in *Dream a New Dream*).

We can choose our attitude. The choice we make is more important than our present circumstances, more important than anything that happened in the past, more important than our physical appearance, our self-image, our enemies' oppression, our disease, our suffering. Life is made up of 10 percent circumstance and 90 percent attitude. The greater part—the 90 percent—is ours to choose.

Strategy for Suffering Number Four: Become a Wounded Healer

We can rejoice and give glory to God in the midst of suffering, knowing that this experience will provide us with new ministries, new ways to bring wholeness to others who are broken. Suffering gives us the opportunity to become healers of others—special healers, *wounded healers.*

Our example, our Wounded Healer, was Jesus Christ Himself. We can be imitators of Christ in this too, by using our wounds and sufferings to bring healing to others.

The Wounded Healer by Henri Nouwen has affected my attitude toward suffering more than any other book. In that book Nouwen writes: "All of our witness, all of our service, all our good intention for Christ will never be perceived as authentic until it comes from a heart that is wounded." Nouwen's challenge is this: We must learn to take our cancer, our broken relationships, our low self-esteem, our sensitivity, or whatever our brokenness is, and let God transform it. We must become so open and vulnerable with others about those wounds that they can be used as a source of healing power in broken lives.

Let me give you an example from the life of a good friend of ours. Diane Schmidt is a wounded healer. After suffering a sore throat for a period of weeks, Diane went to a doctor who told her she needed to have her tonsils out. One tonsil was removed and was found to be tumorous. The tumor was malignant, and there was a question as to whether or not the malignancy was spreading throughout her lymphatic system.

I sat with Diane in the hospital room when the doctor came in and outlined her alternatives. In a very loving but forthright manner Diane said, "I want you to know first of all, Doctor, that I am a Christian. Because I'm a Christian, my life is in God's hands and I know that even if this cancer ends my life I will live with Him in eternity."

The doctor then went through the options, the best of which seemed to be immediate surgery. She said, "That's fine, let's do the surgery." The next day, Diane spent ten hours in surgery. I was with her mother and sister in the waiting room through those ten hours. Finally the physician came out and said, "I just want you to know that in all the years I've been a surgeon, I have never seen a woman with such character in suffering as Diane."

Today, because she is willing to be open to others about her wounds and to let those wounds be a source of healing power to others, Diane Schmidt ministers to other people who have cancer.

All of us have cancers, all of us have wounds, all of us have brokenness. The call of God is to be so open and vulnerable about those wounds that they can be used as a source of healing to other brokenhearted people. Who ministers to the alcoholic better than a reformed alcoholic? Who ministers to the cancer patient better than someone who has struggled with the same disease? Think of the struggles and trials you have undergone, or that you are undergoing now. Who is better equipped to understand and minister to someone who hurts in those same ways than you?

If you hide your hurt and hold it inside, it becomes unbearable pain, serving no purpose, comforting no one, helping no one. But if you learn to turn your suffering into service to others, you can rejoice and give glory to God.

What are your wounds? Where is your brokenness? How can the trials in your life be transformed into healing power, a brand-new ministry to others? It's one of the great, glorious ironies of the Christian life that only through our wounds can we be used as channels of God's healing. Only through our brokenness can we bring others to wholeness in the midst of a broken world.

One of my favorite authors is Elisabeth Elliot, the widow of missionary Jim Elliot. In 1956, Jim Elliot and four other men had a vision to reach the Auca Indians in Ecuador for Jesus Christ. At that time, the Aucas had not only not been reached with the gospel, but as far as is known, they had not been contacted by the outside world at all. What was known was that, a few years earlier, several oil company employees had been slaughtered in the area by this same tribe.

Jim Elliot and his friends prayed and planned for weeks until the time finally came for them to make contact with the Aucas. They flew to the tribe's village and, before landing, dropped gifts to show their friendly intentions. Then they landed their small plane on the river, and waded ashore, courageously obedient to the leading of their Lord.

Elisabeth waited by the short-wave radio for news of her husband and his adventure for Christ. Finally, the news came: all five missionaries had been slaughtered at the river's edge by the Aucas. As she listened, the first message that came to Elisabeth Elliot's heart was this, spoken by God through the prophet Isaiah:

"When you pass through the waters,
   I will be with you;
And through the rivers,
   they shall not overflow you.
When you walk through the fire,
   you shall not be burned,
Nor shall the flame scorch you.
   For I am the LORD your God . . ." (Is. 43:2–3).

Notice, this promise begins "*when* you pass through the waters," not *if*. And God's assurance is an unequivocal, reliable "I will be with you."

After a number of years living as a widow, Elisabeth Elliot married Addison Leitch (a man who had a great influence on my life during the time he was the assistant to the president of Tarkio College). Shortly after their marriage, Addison Leitch contracted two distinct, unrelated, and extremely painful forms of cancer.

As she cared for her husband, Elisabeth first prayed for help to get through each week. Then she began to pray that God would help her to get through each day. Finally, she knew that even that was unrealistic, and she began to pray that God would help her get through each hour. The work and the grief for her suffering husband became so great that when it was 9:00 A.M., to think about 10:00 A.M. was unbearable.

One day as she was studying the Scriptures, she read the incident of Jesus and the little boy who came to Him with five loaves and two fish (see John 6:1–14). According to the account, the disciples wanted to turn the boy away, saying, "What good will such a pittance do with so great a multitude as five thousand people?" But Jesus called the little boy to Him. He took the little pittance and prayed for it and blessed it. He transformed it and fed a multitude.

Elisabeth realized this was what she had to do with her suffering. She had to offer it to God and let Him pray for it and bless it and let it be transformed so that it could be a ministry to others. This realization changed her whole perspective on suffering.

Today, in her books and public appearances, Elisabeth Elliot ministers as a wounded healer to thousands of hurting people. On one of the occasions I heard her speak, she joyfully quoted these words from *The Son's Cause* by Father Van: "To turn a small trial into a trough of self-pity is to make it and ourselves still more petty. To share it with Him is to turn it, however small it may be, into a thing of grandeur—a giving of love to others."

What does God want to do with our suffering and our brokenness? He wants to take it, transform it, and use it as a ministry to others. Thus we rejoice in the midst of our suffering, knowing that suffering produces endurance, endurance produces character, and character produces hope.

And hope will never disappoint us.

4. TO WALK AND NOT FAINT

God Always Heals. . . If—

Those who wait on the LORD
Shall renew their strength;
They shall mount up with wings like eagles,
They shall run and not be weary,
They shall walk and not faint (Is. 40:31).

Do you know the conversion story of C. S. Lewis? Lewis—author, scholar, and apologist—was once an angry atheist. He was not simply an indifferent nonbeliever, not just an unconvinced agnostic. Before his struggle with the Holy Spirit (which he ultimately and happily lost), Lewis was an angry, antagonistic, confirmed atheist.

The events and influences that led Lewis into atheism were many, but one of the strongest and most deeply felt of those influences was a struggle with suffering that he witnessed firsthand at a very young age.

He was only nine years old as he watched his beloved mother suffering, wasting away in the grip of cancer. He later wrote in *Surprised by Joy* that "when her case was pronounced hopeless I remembered what I had been taught; that prayers offered in faith would be granted. I accordingly set myself to produce by will power a firm belief that my prayers for her recovery would be successful."

But though the boy Lewis prayed to what he pictured as a

"magician-God" with all the faith he could muster, there was no miracle.

As Lewis grew older, he turned to intellectual pursuits and away from the "magician-God" who had been either unwilling or unable to heal his mother. But God would not let the young atheist go. "You must picture me," wrote Lewis,

> alone in my room, night after night, feeling—whenever my mind lifted even a second from my work—the steady, unrelenting approach of Him whom I so earnestly desired not to meet. That which I greatly feared had at last come upon me. In the Trinity Term of 1929, I gave in, and admitted that God was God, and knelt and prayed: perhaps, that night, the most dejected and reluctant convert in all England (from *Surprised by Joy*).

But the struggle of faith—especially faith through times of trial and suffering—was not over for Lewis. Late in his life, he was again to lose the joy in his life—his wife, Joy Davidman Lewis. Like his mother, Lewis's wife died a painful, lingering death from cancer. As she was suffering and dying, Lewis did what any of us would do and, in fact, what he had done as a nine-year-old boy at the bedside of his mother. He prayed for divine intervention, for a dramatic miracle of healing, but there was no miracle of healing.

Shortly after the death of his wife, Lewis began to write down his honest questions and feelings in a personal journal. These notes were later collected and published under a pseudonym; he was reluctant to publish them under his own name because they contained many troubled, angry, Joblike questions. Though no longer an atheist, Lewis was again angry with God. This book was not published under Lewis's own name until after his death; it is called *A Grief Observed*.

Written toward the end of Lewis's life, *A Grief Observed* was his second book on the problem of trial and suffering; his first, written in 1940 (comparatively early in his Christian life), was *The Problem of Pain.* In *A Grief Observed* Lewis wrote that he felt God had let him down. Before his wife's death, he prayed for a miracle; no miracle came. After her death, he prayed for victory and consolation; he felt only loneliness and grief. The questions and doubts he expressed are harsh, bitter, and deeply troubled.

But toward the end of the book, Lewis began to see an error in his thinking. He realized that God had not let him down, that his relationship with Christ was strong. He also saw that he had been given false expectations by many well-meaning Christian friends about what the Bible does and does not promise in a time of trial, illness, or grief.

A key truth for us to grasp about healing is that disillusion is always the child of illusion. In life, in faith, in suffering, in disease, we will always become disillusioned if we have been taught an illusion. And we will lead others down a pathway of disillusionment if we teach them an illusion about what the Bible really says about healing.

The Bible contains some bold and amazing promises about the healing touch of God in times of trial. The Bible promises that God will be a very present help; that the Lord will renew our strength; that by the stripes and wounds of Jesus Christ we are healed; that if we ask, it shall be given. These are not illusionary statements; these are the rock-hard promises of God. Yet on the surface, they don't seem to square with the experiences C. S. Lewis faced, and they may not seem to square with the experience you are facing right now. You may be praying for release and healing from an illness or trial—either yours or that of someone you love—and the trial goes on and on, and your prayer for healing seems to go unanswered. How can we reconcile these crises of suffering with the promises of the Bible?

We can begin by understanding that God works in many ways; He cannot be boxed in, nor can He be steered along one single avenue of healing. We see in Scripture and in life that His healing touch takes many different forms.

I want to suggest three different forms that His healing love may take, three different ways in which God lovingly touches and transforms our trials and pain. For each of these forms of healing, I will give you a biblical example and a contemporary example. My purpose here is to show you that God *always* heals—*if*. If we are faithful and flexible enough to accept the form of healing He has chosen for us or our loved ones, we will be healed.

Divine Intervention

Many people have experienced trials of terrible suffering and stress—such as an illness for which there is no known medical cure—and have suddenly seen God radically, dramatically, miraculously break through. This is *divine intervention*.

A biblical example of divine intervention is found in Mark 1:40–45. A leper came on his knees to Jesus and begged Him for healing. He was beyond the medical help of his day. He was alienated socially, but he had faith. "If You are willing," he told Jesus, "You can make me clean." Jesus, filled with compassion, replied, "I am willing." And He touched the man and immediately healed him of his incurable disease in a way that defies medical explanation.

A contemporary example of divine intervention occurred in the life of a friend of mine. A few years ago, she was diagnosed as having cancer. She asked the pastors and elders of our church to come and pray for her to be healed. Following the admonition of James 5:13–16, we went to her home, prayed for her, anointed her with oil, and laid hands on her. A few days later, she went back to the hospital for X-rays. To the bafflement of the doctors, the X-rays revealed that all evidence of her cancer—which had been so clear in the previous set of X-rays—had suddenly disappeared. She had been miraculously healed.

Miracles of healing occur in our time just as they did in the first century. I am an eyewitness. So I have to disagree with a few of my Christian friends who still believe that miracles of healing have passed away, that such miracles were of another era or dispensation.

I also have to give a word of warning: God does not always choose to heal by divine intervention. Moreover, we have to be very careful about our motives when we ask in prayer for this form of healing.

Miracles in the New Testament were always given as a sign. The Bible clearly shows that miracles were used by God as demonstrations of the divinity and authority of Jesus Christ, or of God's love to us, or of His sovereignty. Jesus warned that we should never demand a sign as a further proof, as if to say, "I won't really believe in You, Jesus, unless You perform another healing miracle in my life" (see Matt. 12:38–39; John 4:46–53).

Jesus Christ is not a magician who has to give us proof after proof in order to buy our faith. Biblically, miracles are signs of the grace of God; ultimately, they culminate in the greatest of all miracles, the resurrection of Jesus Christ from the dead. If we are objective and honest in our study of the early church, we see in the book of Acts that the miraculous events at the beginning of the book gradually diminish toward the end. Clearly, there was a lessened emphasis on divine intervention in the first century church. As you read

Luke's account in Acts, or Paul's epistles, you find neither writer bemoaning the fact that miracles are becoming more and more rare.

Some people explain the diminished emphasis on miracles by saying, "Well, that's because the early Christians gradually had less faith." I'm convinced that the miracles did not diminish as the early Christians' faith diminished. No, the miracles diminished because they had more faith. They no longer needed miraculous healing—divine intervention—to attest to the reality of Jesus Christ in their lives.

Karl Kassulke writes,

> Recently, a well-meaning lady asked me why I hadn't prayed for healing. "Karl, if you would let Him," she said, "the Lord would heal you." I would enjoy walking again someday, and someday when I get to heaven I believe I will. That isn't to make light of healing. After all, God has healed my troubled mind as well as my heart and soul, but I had to remind this lady that I don't have to have a miracle to convince myself or anybody else that I have faith. I know that the Lord is real. I don't need to prove it to anybody.

When we see God heal in a way that defies natural explanation (as in the case of the leper in Mark 1:40–45, or my friend who was miraculously cured of cancer), then we are awed and humbled that God in His power, sovereignty, and compassion has chosen to move in this way. But God does not always choose to act by this means. Let me tell you about a second form of healing.

Partnership

There are times when God chooses not just to work for us, but with us, in partnership with the accepted medical practices of the day. A biblical model of this second kind of healing is found in John 9. There, Jesus and his disciples came upon a man who had been blind since birth. "Rabbi," the disciples asked Him, "who sinned, this man or his parents, that he was born blind?"

Jesus' reply cut through their fatalistic view of life and dispelled the false idea that a specific incidence of suffering is always due to an act of sin: "Neither this man nor his parents sinned," said Jesus, "but [this happened so] that the works of God should be revealed in him."

Then Jesus applied a poultice of mud to the blind man's eyes and instructed him to bathe in the pool of Siloam. (This practice obviously seems ineffectual and archaic compared with modern medicine. But in full accord with the medical practices of that day, the man stepped into the pool, washed the mud from his eyes, and emerged seeing for the first time in his life.) Jesus Christ, the Great Physician, worked in partnership with the medical remedy of that time, and provided the power behind the treatment that gave sight to the blind man.

Throughout the ministry of Jesus Christ, we see that He not only preached—He loved, He showed compassion, He cared for human need and suffering. That is why Jesus healed the leper, why He touched the blind man, why He ministered to the woman who was bleeding internally. And why He singled out the little children and called them to Him.

The very presence of hospitals in Western civilization is rooted in the ministry and compassion of Jesus Christ. Before Christ, the prevailing view of life was fatalism; it said, "If you suffer, it's because of your sin. Therefore, you don't deserve medical care. You deserve your suffering." Jesus dispelled this fatalistic view of life, saying, "I've taken your sin onto Myself. I've died on the cross for your sin. Now you must respond in a new way toward suffering. No longer should you let suffering or illness defeat you. No longer should you passively sit by and allow suffering to destroy you and those around you. I want you to fight suffering—fight it on every front."

As Christians, we must fight disease and suffering in every way open to us, always asking God for His help. That's partnership with God, the second form of healing. There is a point where we are responsible, where we cannot expect God's healing if we are not willing to work in cooperation with Him.

Let's not confine our discussion of healing only to illness or physical injury. There is little point in glibly offering prayers for healing in our marriage relationship if we are not willing to work in partnership with God to see that healing begin. There is little point in praying, "Help me, Lord, to have a better self-image," or, "Help me, Lord, to become more mature in Christ," or, "Help me, Lord, to have healing in a broken relationship," if we are not willing to work in partnership with God to bring that healing about.

A contemporary example of healing by partnership between God and medicine comes from my own family. In the first chapter, I told you about our daughter Rachael, who was born prematurely, critically ill, and was not expected to live. When the doctors told us how sick Rachael was, we didn't take her home and pray for a healing of dramatic divine intervention. We did everything we could to work in partnership with God to heal our daughter.

We sought the prayers of many people for her life. We had her rushed by ambulance to a special children's hospital where she could receive more specific and intensive infant care. We made over a hundred visits to the hospital, conferring with our doctor, visiting Rachael, and—when she had gained some strength and resistance—putting our hands through the rubber cuffs in the incubator and stroking her (because we learned that even with very premature children, stroking and touching is a ministry of love that encourages healing and growth). We sought the best Christian doctors and nurses and worked in partnership with them, and eventually—by God's grace and power and the expertise of the doctors—Rachael was healed.

Rachael's healing through our partnership with medicine was no less miraculous, was no less an act of God's grace and power, than the extraordinary healing of my friend who was cured of cancer. And the healing of the blind man by collaborative means was no less a miracle than the extraordinary divine intervention that cleansed the leper. They were two different forms of healing, but they had a similar result.

Yet God does not always choose to heal by one of those two means. There is a third form of healing, the form that is inevitably the most difficult for us to accept.

God's Sufficient Grace

There are certain times when disease, trials, or heartaches are given to us and they are not going to be taken away. They're going to have to be endured, but they don't have to defeat us.

The apostle Paul was able to say triumphantly, "We are more than conquerors through Him who loved us" (Rom. 8:37), even though he suffered through a long period of physical pain and struggle in his own life. In 2 Corinthians 12, Paul referred to this period of suffering as "a thorn in the flesh." And though he didn't say exactly what this thorn in the flesh was, we know it had a hindering effect on his ministry and a debilitating effect on his life. Because Paul felt that this suffering made him less effective as a man of God, he went to God the Father three times in prayer, begging

God, "Please heal me! Please remove this thorn in the flesh!"

But God answered, "Paul, I will give you My grace, which is sufficient for this time of trial. I will give you My strength in your weakness" (see 2 Cor. 12:7–10).

The Greek word our English Bible renders "thorn" literally means "stake," a thing that pierces and brings pain. So Paul was saying, "There is a stake in my body, causing me physical pain. I've asked God three times to take it away, but my suffering is still with me." Although we can't be sure what Paul's thorn in the flesh was, some have suggested it was lasting damage from all the scourging he endured. Others suggest it was an incurable disease, malaria, epilepsy, or some other malady. My own suspicion is that Paul was gradually going blind.

In his letter to the Galatians, Paul wrote, "You know that because of physical infirmity I preached the gospel to you at the first. And my trial which was in my flesh you did not despise or reject, but received me as an angel of God, even as Christ Jesus. . . . I bear you witness that. . .you would have plucked out your own eyes and given them to me" (Gal. 4:13–15). And in chapter 6, he writes, "See with what large letters I have written to you with my own hand!" (v. 11). Paul, who usually dictated his epistles to a "secretary," concluded the Galatian letter in his own large scrawl, writing in the kind of big letters that a person gradually going blind might use. Perhaps Paul never fully recovered from his blinding encounter with Jesus Christ on the Damascus road. We can only guess.

Whatever Paul's infirmity, whatever his thorn in the flesh, we know that Paul went before the Father and prayed for healing. We know the form of healing God gave to Paul was His sufficient grace, His strength in Paul's weakness. Did this gift of grace turn out to be the best for Paul, and for God's glory? In his life and epistles, we see that Paul became even more dependent on God, and an even more faithful follower of Jesus Christ. He was able not only to declare, but also to model for us a bold statement: When I am weak, then I am strong. For the power of Christ dwells in me (see 2 Cor. 12:7–10).

There are certain trials that we are not going to be able to change. We are going to have to allow them to change us. This third form of healing is as valid an expression of the miraculous healing love of God as the first two. If we tell people only about divine intervention or partnership healing, they will become disillusioned, either gradually or suddenly, as some trial comes into their lives and is not taken away.

Each of us needs to be humble and teachable in the face of what the Scriptures clearly set forth. We must have the integrity and boldness to tell others, as the Bible clearly tells us, that God's healing touch sometimes takes the form of sufficient grace, His strength in our weakness. If we have that integrity and humility as we counsel others about God's healing love, then we will no longer dole out hollow promises and illusions about healing; rather, we will have ministered the whole Word of God.

Laura Claypool, the daughter of author-pastor John Claypool, was only eight years old when she was diagnosed as having acute leukemia, a form of cancer that attacks the white blood cells. Laura's father immediately did what any father would do: he went to his knees in prayer, asking God to heal his daughter and spare her life.

The entire congregation of John Claypool's church joined in praying for Laura, by faith believing that Jesus would heal her, for they had seen other dramatic healings in the life of their church. In one of his sermons before that congregation, John Claypool shared about his struggle of faith through Laura's struggle for life:

There were times when Laura was hurting so intensely that she had to bite on a rag and used to beg me to pray to God to take away that awful pain. I would kneel down beside her bed and pray with all the faith and conviction of my soul, and nothing would happen except the pain continued to rage on. Or again when she asked me in the dark of the night, "When will this leukemia go away?"

I answered, "I don't know, darling, but we are doing everything we know to make that happen."

Then she said, "Have you asked God when it will go away?"

And I said, "Yes, you heard me pray to Him many times."

But she persisted, "What did He say? When did He say it would go away?"

And I had to admit to myself that He had not said a word. I had done a lot of talking and praying and pleading, but the response of the heavens had been silence (from *Tracks of a Fellow Struggler*).

John Claypool prayed. And the congregation prayed. They looked anxiously for a sign of healing in Laura's life, either by divine intervention or by partnership between God and the best efforts that medical science could offer. But the battle was not resolved by either of these means. Laura Claypool fought a courageous battle for eighteen months, and on one snowy midwinter night, her struggle ended. The form of healing God chose for Laura was to call her home to be with Him.

For a long time afterward, John Claypool agonized over the memory of his little daughter's pain and death. But in the midst of that abysmal grief, he experienced healing from the Lord, God's grace in a grieving father's weakness. He began to see in a new and profound way that all of life is a gift. A few months after Laura's death, John Claypool was able to speak these words before his congregation:

> Everywhere I turn I am surrounded by reminders of Laura —things we did together, things she said, things she loved. And in the presence of the reminders, I have two alternatives: either to dwell on the fact that she has been taken away or to focus on the wonder that she was given at all (from *Tracks of a Fellow Struggler*).

Those are the only two alternatives any of us have. You may have lost a loved one, possibly a beautiful little child like Laura Claypool. Or perhaps you have seen your children grow up and move away to a distant city. Perhaps you yourself have just moved to a new place, far from family and friends, and you're lonelier than you've ever been before. Perhaps you've just been forsaken by someone who promised to love you for the rest of your life. Whatever your struggle, you really have only two alternatives regarding these loved ones and your own loneliness or grief: you can either dwell on the fact that they have been taken away, or you can focus on the wonder that by the grace of God they were given at all.

I really believe that the only way out of the valley of sorrows is to climb the mountain of gratitude. We have to realize that all of life, for however long we have it, is a gift. We cannot earn it. Life and family and friends are gifts that have been given to us, despite our sin, by the grace of God.

A recent best-selling book is *When Bad Things Happen To Good People*. I wonder if the real issue isn't really, "Why do good things happen to bad people?" for all of us have sinned, and we deserve no good gifts from the Father at all.

When we start to see our loved ones as unmerited gifts, then we no longer want to clutch them, smother them, possess them. Instead, we hold them with open hands, knowing they are gifts from God. This one truth has helped me more than any other in my response to loss and grief.

One of the first verses of Scripture my parents taught me was Isaiah 40:31:

> "But those who wait on the LORD
> Shall renew their strength;
> They shall mount up with wings like eagles,
> They shall run and not be weary,
> They shall walk and not faint."

There will come times of trial in our lives when we will pray for healing and deliverance, and we'll wait upon the Lord, and the Lord will dramatically intervene. He will miraculously renew our strength and lift us out of our trial so that we soar like eagles, praising God as we leave our pain or sorrow below.

There will also come times when we will have to work in partnership with God to bring about healing; we'll be able to run with God, not becoming weary, doing all we can together with the Great Physician, and thanking Him for His grace.

There will also come times when all we are able to do in life is walk and not faint. We won't be able to soar; we won't be able to run. We will have to withstand a trial we cannot change. But at least we will be able to walk and, by the grace of God, not faint. That is the witness of John Claypool and C. S. Lewis and the apostle Paul. As they endured suffering, or stood by suffering loved ones, they could do nothing but walk, put one foot in front of the other, without fainting. Out of their struggles against the terrible trials in their lives—struggles often filled with honest, angry, doubting questions—God was able to bring them forth with a tougher, more reliable, proven faith.

What trial are you struggling with right now? God has

given you a promise of healing for that trial, and He will choose one of three ways to bring that healing about.

Those who wait upon the Lord shall renew their strength. At times they shall mount up with wings as eagles. At other times they shall run and not be weary. But at least they are always going to be able to walk and not faint. Even if we are powerless to change our burden of sorrow, pain, or grief, we can still stand through the sufficient grace of Jesus Christ.

5. OUR GOOD—OR GOD'S?

The Best Loved, Least Understood Verse in the Bible

And we know that all things work together for good to those who love God, to those who are the called according to His purpose (Rom. 8:28).

I was thumbing through a popular Christian magazine recently, when an advertisement caught my attention. It featured a photograph of a gold-plated bracelet charm sculpted with a representation of the face of Christ. The advertising text read something like this:

"Overcome all your problems! Enjoy success, good fortune, and radiant health! Jesus has been bringing happiness and prosperity to millions for almost 2,000 years. Now you can carry Jesus with you wherever you go with this lovely 24K gold-plated charm in the likeness of Christ. Order now! Satisfaction guaranteed!"

Discerning Christians may note the similarity between such a "good-luck charm" and what the Old Testament calls "graven images." Sadly, this attempt to gold-plate the image of Jesus Christ seems only to cheapen it. And while the ad promises happiness and success and good fortune, plus guaranteed satisfaction, God's Word never does.

In fact, I believe that many of us have actually made a gold-plated good-luck charm out of one of the deepest, most beautiful, and most quoted verses in the Bible. That verse is Romans 8:28, "And we know that all things work together for good to those who love God, to those who are the called according to His purpose." What do those words mean to you?

To many, this verse reads much like the words of the good-luck charm ad: "If you love God, you can overcome all your troubles and enjoy happiness and success and good fortune in life—complete satisfaction guaranteed." I believe emphatically that this is *not* what Romans 8:28 is saying. In fact, I'm convinced that such a gold-plated version of this verse does a disservice to the integrity of Scripture and cheapens the gospel of Jesus Christ. It ignores the cost of discipleship and suggests that God is only at work for *our* gain, *our* prosperity, *our* good fortune.

The Most Misunderstood Verse

In Romans 8:28 we have what I believe is the most beloved, but the most misunderstood, verse in the New Testament. Dr. F. F. Bruce, the great Bible scholar and expositor of the Greek New Testament, argues that the subject of the sentence is *God*. If that is true, then the word *good* in the sentence structure must refer to God, not to you and me. Let's look at the verse again in a literal translation from the Greek text: "We know that, in everything, God works for good with those who love Him, who are called according to His purpose." To understand this is to understand Romans 8:28 in a new and completely different way—a way that is more profound, more biblically sound, and more reliably encouraging during times of trial.

God is at work for *His* good in our lives. If we truly love Him, if we make ourselves available to Him, the promise is that God will work for His good, the fulfillment of His eternal plan—not merely for our own temporal gain. Accordingly, most Bible translations and paraphrases totally miss the thrust of Paul's argument. *The Living Bible,* for example, paraphrases Romans 8:28: "We know that all that happens to us is working for our good if we love God...." In skewing the true sense of this verse, in transferring the *good* from God to us, *The Living Bible* (as do many other translations and paraphrases) completely misses the point of the text.

The promise in this passage is not that every single thing in life is for our good. No, the promise is that all things are woven together and working for good—God's good. This is no cheap, hollow promise of financial reward or a life of ease. This is a promise of God's eternal purpose for your life. If you love God and are available to Him, then He can use everything in your life to accomplish His eternal plan of the ages through you.

Does this mean that God doesn't care about your health, your happiness, your finances? Does this mean that God might actually allow you to be crushed by suffering or circumstances so that some greater good for God can occur? No, I want to assure you that God is very much interested in you, your well-being, your happiness, and your finances. But according to the Bible, these are not His primary concerns.

God ultimately desires that we come to know Him. In John 17:3, Jesus says, "And this is eternal life, that they may know You, the only true God, and Jesus Christ whom You have sent."

Romans 8:29 tells us further that God's ultimate purpose for our lives is not good health or financial prosperity or a comfortable life; rather, He deeply desires that we become "conformed to the image of His Son," Jesus Christ. That is God's good; ultimately, it is our good as well—even if it means that we have to pass through difficult trials in order to be conformed to the image of Christ.

God's good is our good, though there will inevitably be many events in our lives that we could never call good, in and of themselves. To pretend everything is by itself good, and to teach others to so pretend, is a perversion of the gospel. The message of Romans 8:28 is that good can come out of the most evil or tragic events that crash into our lives, if we will make ourselves open and available to God. But we must be careful not to confuse God's good with our gain. Romans 8:28 does not promise us prosperity or lifelong good health or freedom from trial and suffering. It promises that God's good will be accomplished even in the midst of our trials.

There is no way we can realistically pretend that separation from a loved one is a good thing. Nor can we say a tragic illness could be a good thing in anyone's life. We ought not pretend that it's a good thing when a friend of ours loses his job or suffers a broken relationship with a family member. But we can respond to those hard places in life in such a way that God is able to work out His will and to accomplish His good purpose. That is the message of Romans 8:28.

Scripture Interprets Scripture

Why has this verse been so widely and tragically misapplied? I believe the principal reason is the common practice of modern interpretation called "proof-texting." Isolated verses of Scripture are quoted without regard to the surrounding text and the correlation of other Scripture, in order to "prove" that a given manmade idea is "biblical." Sadly, many people are deceived into following bogus doctrine and false teachers because, unlike the diligent believers at Berea (see Acts 17:11), they fail to search the Scriptures to see if these things are so.

What, then, is the best way to guard against error in interpreting the Scriptures?

When we study the Scriptures, we must apply a principle Martin Luther called the analogy of faith. Stated simply, the analogy of faith means that Scripture interprets Scripture. For example, if you want to understand what the New Testament teaches on prayer, you do not simply read the verse, "Ask and you shall receive," and stop there, believing you can simply ask for anything and it's yours. You must dig into the Scriptures to get a full overview of what the Old and New Testaments teach. Only then can you begin to understand the full rich biblical truth about prayer.

When we apply this rule to Romans 8:28, it becomes clear that this verse is not the gold-plated good-luck charm that so many claim it to be. Instead, we see that it can only mean one thing: if we are available to God and love Him, then His good plan will be accomplished, even in our most trying and painful circumstances.

You may know Leighton Ford as one of the leaders of the evangelical church in America, as a close associate of Billy Graham, and as a gifted teacher and communicator. Since my years in Minneapolis, I've known Leighton Ford as a friend and as one of the guiding and inspiring influences in my life and ministry. Not long ago, I received a letter from him that told about the death of his twenty-year-old son, Sandy, during surgery. This touching excerpt from that letter expresses the understanding of Romans 8:28 that we all need to have, and the kind of mature Christian character we all want in a time of trial:

> We grieve deeply over Sandy's death. The loss has been unexpected and far more crushing than we can express. But we know that he is with the Lord whom he loved and served. His life was not cut short, but completed. . . . The

day before Sandy's surgery I prayed, "God, be good to my boy." God has been good, though not as we expected. We look forward to understanding more of why He chose to show His goodness in this way.

Was the loss of his son a good thing to Leighton Ford? No, of course not. The first thing he talks about is the grief, the crushing and inexpressible sense of loss. But through this inexplicable trial, he expresses faith and confidence in God's goodness—a goodness that is difficult to understand at such times, but a goodness that is promised to us in Romans 8:28.

God is at work, weaving all the circumstances of our lives together into a purposeful, glorious pattern. He uses our joyful circumstances and our painful circumstances for one all-important purpose. And what is that purpose? Look again at Romans 8:29: "For whom He foreknew, He also predestined to be conformed to the image of His Son, that He might be the firstborn among many brethren." Don't be scared off by that word *predestined*. It simply means that God made a decision about you ahead of time; that you as a Christian should be conformed to the image of His Son. This is the goal of the Christian life—to be conformed to the image of Jesus Christ.

Superconquerors!

In Romans 8:31–39, Paul raised his magnificent, unanswerable questions: "If God is for us, who can be against us?...It is God who justifies. Who is he who condemns?...Who shall separate us from the love of Christ?" Paul's answer—*nothing* can separate us from the love of Christ. He listed a whole catalogue of sufferings and trials—tribulation, distress, persecution, famine, nakedness, peril, sword (that is, martyrdom)—none of which can separate us from God's love.

In the verses that follow Romans 8:28, Paul categorically stated that we may encounter some of the worst and most painful circumstances imaginable (including the death-dealing sword of martyrdom itself). He said that there is no "complete satisfaction guaranteed," no promise of ease, success, and good fortune in this life. But even so, Paul declared that the deepest tragedy is not deep enough to separate us from the love of Christ.

The reality of this call to the will of God comes through even clearer as we consider the audience for Paul's Roman letter. Remember the apostle was not writing to comfortable, affluent, socially-oriented Christian people. He was writing to Christians in captivity and oppression, living in Rome under the cruel, irrational reign of Nero. Believers were being slaughtered for their faith by the hundreds in Rome. Paul anticipated their questions: "Paul, what about our distress? What about the sword of imperial Rome? Will martyrdom separate me from Jesus Christ?" Paul answered resoundingly, triumphantly, "No! Nothing will separate you from His love! In fact, because you love Him, because you are called according to His purpose, He can use your trying circumstances to produce His good!"

That is why Paul was able to say in verse 37, "In all these things"—in all the trials and sufferings he listed in verse 35—"we are more than conquerors...." That phrase is five words in English, but one word in the original Greek: *hyper-nikomen. Hyper* means "super"; *nikomen* means "we conquer." What Paul said, in effect, was this: "In all things, *we are superconquerors* through Him who loved us!"

The *good* of Romans 8:28 is not anything so small and temporal as the popular goal of "happiness and success and good fortune." Rather, the *good* of this passage is a magnificent, lofty good—God's supergood. We become superconquerors when we yield to His will and become obedient, willing, living sacrifices on the altar of His plan.

We can be assured that, in everything, God works for His good with those who love Him, who are called according to His purpose. Whatever happens, whatever trial or affliction we are called on to endure in this life, we are superconquerors through God who loved us and gave His Son to die for us. Nothing can ever separate us from that amazing love.

Four Spiritual Myths

I believe the many misapplications of Romans 8:28 to suffering center around four myths, four areas of misunderstanding about this verse.

Myth Number One: If you love God, everything will work out for your gain. It will not. We do a great disservice when we try to induce non-Christians into receiving Christ on the basis that everything good will suddenly come their way as a result. A gospel of "successful living through salvation" can only lead to disillusionment in the life of the new Christian.

The clear witness of Scripture is that the abundant Christian life often entails losing everything for the sake of the kingdom of God, and in suffering becoming spiritually rich. "What things were gain to me, these I have counted loss for Christ," said Paul. "I have suffered the loss of all things, and count them as rubbish, that I may gain Christ" (Phil. 3:7–8; see also Matt. 16:24–26; Luke 18:18–23; 2 Cor. 8:1–15).

Myth Number Two: Every problem you will ever have is addressed in the Bible. This is not true. Although the Bible contains many specific guidelines and broad principles for our behavior and decisions, it is by no means a divine "answer book" for all of earth's problems. It is unwise for us to make sweeping statements about specific problems in life, as if the Bible contains a neat solution for each one. Many times in life we will face a crisis or a decision, and there will be no clear direction given in God's Word. At such times we have an opportunity to live by raw faith, trusting in the lordship of Jesus Christ and seeking the guidance of the Holy Spirit.

Myth Number Three: If you have problems, you are unspiritual. No. The reality is that if you are having a problem, it's because you're human. We do a great disservice to our Christian brothers and sisters when we imply, whether subtly or overtly, that they are lacking in their fellowship with God if they are struggling or hurting. In Galatians we are commanded to bear one another's burdens; instead, we often increase each other's burdens by making each other feel guilty for their pain or anguish.

Myth Number Four: According to Romans 8:28, God's primary objective is our happiness. This is not God's primary objective. Much of the preaching we hear in American churches today is essentially human-centered, not God-centered. The message we often hear is about how God can bring you prosperity, success, and good fortune, rather than about what we can do for God if we take up the cross in obedience to His lordship.

The Scriptures are totally clear on God's primary objective, relative to each of us as Christians, and His eternal purpose is not my happiness or yours. Certainly, He is interested in our happiness, as He is interested in our health and our physical well-being. But God's central, overriding concern for each of us is that we be conformed into the image of Jesus Christ. That process of becoming Christlike happens both through happy times and through deep sadness. It happens through joy, and through grief and sorrow. It happens through vigorous good health, and through periods of pain, disease, and weakness.

Not long ago, I confided in a friend about some difficult times I was having in my life. After I got through listing some of my specific burdens, I shook my head and said exactly what I felt at that moment: "I just want to get on with what God's called me to, yet I feel so frustrated! Why am I having so many trials piled onto me just now?"

My friend thought for a moment, then said, "I think you're going through some hard times in your life because God wants to conform you into the image of His Son. He wants to make you more and more like Jesus." We need to see all our trials in light of that process—from the petty frustrations of the keys being locked in the car or of the plumbing backed up, to the great and awful tragedies of life.

Romans 8:28 issues a challenge that each of us must answer. Do you love God enough to pray this prayer? "Lord, I'm willing for You to do anything in my life that will accomplish Your good and Your ultimate purpose, no matter what it costs me."

Some time ago, I received a letter from an acquaintance of mine, a heartbreaking but inspiring letter that demonstrates, better than anything I can say, what it means to have a realistic and biblical understanding of God's goodness in times of trial. Here is a portion of that letter:

> It's been about two months since we discovered that our two-year-old daughter Lisa has cancer. Of course, things aren't back to normal. They never will be. Evil has won for the moment, and the pain inflicted by its victory is no less painful because we know that God—even in this—can use it for His good. Joe Bayly once said to us, "Never doubt in the darkness what God has shown you in the light." We haven't, and our prayer is that Lisa can have courage to see her way through this—and that we can have courage in the midst of it too.

This young father's prayer is the prayer of Romans 8:28. It's a prayer that believes that God has the power to heal miraculously—but accepts that God may choose to take them through a crisis instead of out of the crisis. It's a prayer not for escape from trial, but for strength to confront the trial squarely by faith.

This is also the prayer of Acts 4. There, the early Christians were being threatened with death for proclaiming Jesus Christ. How did they respond? They prayed: "Now, Lord, look on their threats, and grant to Your servants"—what, escape from persecution and death? No—"that with all *boldness* they may speak Your word" (Acts 4:29, italics mine). They sought from God a way through their crisis, not a way out.

For centuries, Christians have been meeting that challenge, paying the cost of discipleship, sacrificing their personal security and comfort for the sake of the kingdom of God. William Carey probably didn't feel very good about leaving the comfort of his home to go to Burma to bear witness for Jesus Christ; he went in obedience, for God's good. Dietrich Bonnhoeffer probably didn't see "happiness and success and good fortune" in his future as he voluntarily left the safety of Union Theological Seminary in New York to return to Hitler's Third Reich and die at the hands of the Nazis; he did it for God's good. Jim Elliot probably didn't feel very good for himself and his young wife as he left her behind at a mission station in Ecuador and flew off to a martyr's death at the hands of the Auca Indians; he was martyred for God's good.

In less dramatic but equally real ways, you and I have to decide every day of our lives, "Am I living for my good—or God's?" It's a choice between seeing God's plan as a paltry good-luck charm for our own gain, or being faithful to the full witness of Scripture and living life for His good, surrendered and totally available to Him for His vast eternal purpose, no matter what the price, no matter how great the challenge.

You and I have a wonderful assurance that everything in our lives, woven together by God, can be used by Him to accomplish His grand, eternal purpose—if we make ourselves available to Him. Can you imagine a more awesome, thrilling challenge than that?

"Lord, Let Me Keep the Cancer. . ."

Tom Skinner shared with me the story of his friend Don. One day, Don noticed that he had a growth on his left ear. He went to a doctor, who diagnosed the growth as a tumor, potentially malignant. The doctor scheduled a biopsy for the following day.

Don went home from the doctor's office and started reading his Bible, especially Romans 8. As he studied the passage, he went back again and again to verse 28, struggling to discover the real significance of that promise for his own trial. Suddenly, he realized for the first time that if he made himself available to God, God's good would be accomplished in his life, regardless of whether it felt good or not.

Then Don knelt and prayed, "Lord Jesus, I know you are the Great Physician, and I know you can heal me of this tumor." Most of us would stop there, but Don went on, praying, "But Lord, if you can get more good out of my life—more of *Your* good—by allowing me to have cancer, then I would like to keep the cancer."

The next day, the hospital tests confirmed that the tumor was malignant. Don had cancer.

During Don's first week in the hospital, he was able, by the power of the Holy Spirit, to win his hospital roommate to the Lord. That young man is now a missionary in South

America, winning scores of other people to Jesus Christ and ministering to poor, hungry children. Don got to know the nurse's aide and shared with her the love of Jesus Christ. Today she is a registered nurse and a believer, ministering not only to the physical needs of patients, but to their emotional and spiritual needs as well. Don got to know a man down the hall during his hospital stay. That man was one of the most influential businessmen in America; today he serves Jesus Christ because of Don's obedience and bold witness.

There is a prosthetic ear where Don's natural ear used to be. He wears that artificial ear for God's glory. If you were to ask Don if he would exchange that artificial left ear for normal hearing again, he'd say, "Not on your life! Because I was willing to live for God's good, there are people scattered literally around this country and in South America who are hearing the good news of Jesus Christ."

Each of us would like to see results like that in our own lives. But we can't expect to see such results unless we are willing to love God enough to say, "Lord, I'm willing for You to use any circumstance in my life to achieve Your purpose—no matter what it costs me." Why must we respond this way to God? Paul gave us the answer in Romans 8:29: so that we might be conformed to the image of Christ.

"It Is Well With My Soul . . ."

You may never have heard of H. G. Spafford, but you have probably heard—and even sung—the words he wrote over a century ago:

> When peace, like a river, attendeth my way,
> When sorrows like sea billows roll;
> Whatever my lot, Thou hast taught me to say,
> It is well, it is well with my soul.

Spafford wrote these words after the loss of his two daughters, who were drowned at sea in a shipwreck. The words *sorrows like sea billows* are no mere figure of speech; these words were penned by a grieving father who saw the sea billows literally crash into his life and sweep away his only two children. This hymn is the only hymn Spafford ever wrote, but it eloquently expresses the heart of a man who was becoming conformed into the image of Christ.

Romans 8:28 and 29 are inseparable; together, those verses form one mighty truth. Everything in life can be used for God's good, *if*—if we are available, if we are willing to demonstrate a kind of maturity and character that the world does not understand, if we are willing to be conformed to the image of Christ.

6. ARE YOU A HEALING AGENT?

You Can Be a Channel for God's Healing Power

Bear one another's burdens, and so fulfill the law of Christ (Gal. 6:2).

A friend of mine, a pastor of a church on the West Coast, told me about a woman in his congregation. We'll call her Ruth. For many years, Ruth had been very active in the church, giving great amounts of time and energy as the church's Christian Education Director. Outwardly, she was a model of industrious good cheer and efficiency. Inwardly, she was falling apart.

Ruth had become severely depressed. Because of her depression, she quit her job and her work in the church. She withdrew from all of her friendships and social contacts, and began to take large quantities of tranquilizers that her physician prescribed. Desperate for help in putting her mind and emotions back together again, she sought help from a psychiatrist who was trained in Freudian psychoanalysis and occasionally from her pastor.

During this time, my friend received a call to pastor a church in another city. He agreed to accept that call, but before he left he felt he should do all he could to help Ruth find some way out of her depression. He started by calling Ruth's psychiatrist.

"I can understand your concern," said the psychiatrist to my friend, "but you have to accept the fact that there is absolutely nothing we can do for Ruth. She's in a state of deep depression, and it's my opinion that she will remain in that depression for the rest of her life. I believe you have done all you can. No one ever will be able to really help Ruth."

What would you have done in my friend's place? Would you have taken the psychiatrist's advice and written Ruth off as "terminally depressed," doomed to a life of crushing despondency, relieved (or deadened) only by mind-numbing drugs? Isn't there some way Ruth can be helped?

Most of us believe that the best thing to do when a troubled person comes to us is to refer them to a professional—a psychiatrist, a psychologist, a clergyman. Without minimizing the contributions that can often be made in certain cases by a trained counselor (especially one who is sensitive to the leading of the Holy Spirit), I believe there is another alternative, a biblical and practical alternative—and for many troubled people, a better alternative. As a pastor, I believe God has gifted the laity (ordinary committed Christians) to be His healing agents, potentially the most effective healing agents in our whole society.

My friend, Ruth's pastor, also believed this to be true. So what did he do in response to the psychiatrist's grim prognosis? He would not acknowledge hopelessness. He decided to refer Ruth to one of a number of house churches within his congregation.

This house church was not merely a weekly Bible study; it was a group of eight or ten people who had committed themselves to each other to study the Bible together, to pray for each other and support each other, to be open, honest, and sensitive to each other, and to hold all sharing within the group in strict confidence. They shared each other's burdens, not just once a week but throughout the week. The concept was modeled on the close community and deep commitment of the believers of the New Testament church. It was not a substitute church, but an important part of the life of the church, encouraged and overseen by the church's pastor.

The people in Ruth's house church were told nothing about her depression or any other special needs; they knew only what was readily apparent: she was lonely and she needed help.

Three months after joining that house church, Ruth was completely off prescribed drugs. Within six months, she had returned to work. Though she had been written off as a hopeless emotional cripple by her psychiatrist, today she experiences the wholeness that can come through a vital personal relationship with Jesus Christ and with other Christian brothers and sisters.

I believe Ruth's story symbolizes the kind of revolutionary transformation that can take place in thousands of broken lives—if we will only be obedient in applying scriptural principles to our lives, our lifestyles, and our relationships.

Upgrading the Church

I want to make it clear that I'm not trying to downgrade the professional counselors and therapists. Today, in fact, there are many professional counselors, including many Christian counselors, who are challenging the conventional Freudian approach to psychiatry. My goal is not to downgrade the professionals, but to upgrade the church—caring, sensitive, committed Christian lay people who are willing, through the power of the Holy Spirit, to be true healing agents to the brokenhearted people in our society.

As Christians, we have to act emotionally and volitionally on what we intellectually say we believe. The promised

Comforter, the Holy Spirit, has come into us, and He seeks to make a difference in us as we seek to minister to others in His name and by His power.

In John 11, we see the amazing story of Jesus, the Great Physician, raising Lazarus from the dead. After He gives new life to Lazarus, He turns to the friends and family of Lazarus—who still stands bound in his graveclothes—and He says, "Now, you unbind him. Set Lazarus free." I think this is an analogy of the responsibility that Jesus Christ has given each of us as Christians: in the church we are to unbind each other, to set each other free.

Only Jesus Christ can redeem us, can save us, can move us from death into life. But once Jesus Christ has given new life to someone who was dead in sin, He turns to us, the family of faith, and says, "Now, you unbind him. Set him free." Jesus Christ has given us as fellow Christians the mutual responsibility of unbinding each other and of helping each other experience His wholeness and healing touch.

How are we to go about the business of unbinding each other, as Christ commanded us? I want to suggest five practical ways.

1. We must involve ourselves with each other.

In the Book of Acts, we see that healing took place in the life of the early church as an outgrowth of relationships —Christians living and sharing together in intense community and worship.

The house churches I wrote about earlier are part of a long tradition going back to the beginning of the church recorded in Acts. In Acts 5:12–16, we see the gathering of what we might call the first house church, literally hundreds of believers meeting daily at Solomon's Porch in Jerusalem, with many more being added all the time. People from the towns all around Jerusalem brought the sick and the emotionally and spiritually tormented for healing, and all of them were healed. Huge numbers of people were made whole within this atmosphere of radical sharing, caring, and community.

I'm not saying that any program, even a house church program, is a cure-all for emotional trouble. God's chosen agency for healing is not programs but people—caring, committed people who are willing to act on what they say they believe. Our counseling of each other, our community and fellowship with each other, and our healing of each other can take place over coffee or pizza, over the phone, at the gym, after a movie, at a hospital bedside, or in a waiting room. All our times together with other Christians can be opportunities for ministering God's healing power.

Though this concept of involvement in each other's lives is contrary to the approach of many professional therapists, the biblical Christian counselor, whether professional or lay, must become involved in caring for the troubled person. Paul Tournier, perhaps the most eminent Christian counselor of our time, writes, "I am convinced that nine out of ten people seeing a psychiatrist do not need one. They need someone who will love them with God's love, and who will take time with them and believe in them—and they *will* get well."

2. We must encourage, guide—and confront.

While we must always affirm the importance of active listening, and we build our credibility and demonstrate our authentic love by really hearing the hurts of troubled people, there is a time when we as Christians must speak. We have to articulate what the Scriptures teach.

There are essentially five Greek words in the New Testament that relate to what we call "counseling":

Parakaleō—"to urge, exhort, encourage, comfort."

Noutheteō—"to admonish, warn, confront."

Paramutheomai—"to encourage, comfort."

Antechomai—"to help, embrace, support, uphold."

Makrothumeō—"to persevere, be patient."

Interestingly, all five words are used by Paul in 1 Thessalonians 5:14: "Now we exhort [*parakaleō*] you, brethren, warn [*noutheteō*] those who are unruly, comfort [*paramutheomai*] the fainthearted, uphold [*antechomai*] the weak, be patient [*makrothumeō*] with all."

Paul also used *parakaleō* in his introduction to 2 Corinthians: "Blessed be the God and Father of our Lord Jesus Christ, the Father of mercies and God of all comfort [*parakaleō*—meaning not only "comfort" but "encouragement"], who comforts us in all our tribulation, that we may be able to comfort those who are in any trouble, with the comfort with which we ourselves are comforted by God" (1:3-4).

In Romans 15:14, Paul said he was "confident concerning you, my brethren, that you also are full of goodness, filled with all knowledge, able also to admonish [*noutheteō*] one another." And in Colossians 3:16, he said, "Let the word of Christ dwell in you richly in all wisdom, teaching and admonishing [*noutheteō*] one another in psalms and hymns and spiritual songs, singing with grace in your hearts to the Lord."

The New Testament commands us to teach, to counsel, to admonish, to encourage, to help, to exhort, to comfort, to guide, to direct, to warn, to confront, to persevere, to be patient.

This issue is especially evident in the area of marital counseling—where a husband and wife are struggling with deep hurts and brokenness in their relationship. Of course, it's important to listen and understand those hurts and struggles before offering any counsel. But often as you listen to what the couple is saying, you hear something like this:

Husband: "Well, I'd be willing to be more of a servant-leader in our home—*if only* my wife would bend a little and adjust herself to my leadership."

Wife: "Well, I'd be willing to recognize his leadership role in our home—*except* he doesn't pattern his servant-leadership after Jesus Christ."

There comes a point where the pastor or lay counselor, after listening and really hearing the hurt, must break in and say, "Hold it. The issue is not your spouse. The issue is your own obedience. The issue is your own will. When you go before the Lord in eternity, you will not go with your spouse. His judgment of you will depend entirely on your own obedience to Christ. Then, as now, what your spouse does or fails to do is purely incidental."

Being a warm, supportive, affirming, caring person toward others is never an end in itself. It is the lordship of Christ, not warmth or affirmation, that is the key ingredient in healing broken relationships. If we want to see this kind of healing take place, then we have to be faithful to the counsel of the New Testament. We must recognize that there comes a time when we must speak.

3. We must emphasize responsibility for the present and the future, not blame for the past.

Whereas some conventional psychiatric approaches to problems place tremendous emphasis on the past (including delving into details of childhood), Christian counseling puts its emphasis on present challenges and future responsibilities to achieve wholeness.

The theory behind past-centered approaches is that by

understanding all the influences, deprivations, and injuries of the past, we can sort through and gain insight into why we feel and act the way we do. Thus we are able to blame others—parents, friends, spouse, environment—for making us the way we are now. Calling this approach "the blame game," psychologist O. Hobart Mower writes, "The success of the blame game seemed complete. Only one thing went wrong: the patients did not get better."

Our instinctive response whenever problems arise is to blame others. We have been well-trained by our cultural surroundings and by our own sin-bent nature to see the speck in the eye of our brother. But in Matthew 7:5 Jesus said to "first remove the plank from your own eye, and then you will see clearly to remove the speck out of your brother's eye." What a graphic illustration! Blame, says Christ, is like a plank of wood in our eyes, blinding us to the solution to our problems.

Psychologist Carl Rogers writes, "Only one kind of troubled person will probably never become whole: the person who blames other people for his problems." Blame never heals; it always hurts. Blame never makes people whole; it always fragments. Blame never affirms; it always attacks. Blame never builds; it always tears down. Blame never solves; it always complicates. Blame never unites; it always divides. Blame only sees the speck in the eye of a brother; it is blind to the plank-size problems that are right before our own eyes.

One tragic result of past-centered, blame-centered psychiatric therapy is that it has helped to create a generation of parent-haters. In the vast majority of cases, we have to admit our parents did the very best they could. But like us they were flawed, prone to sin and mistakes, and limited in their understanding.

You may be thinking, "But you didn't know my parents!

They totally violated their responsibility as parents, and left emotional and psychological scars in me that will never heal!" That may be true. But even so, if you are a biblical Christian—and if you truly want to be healed of those psychological scars—then you have to take the attitude of Joseph.

In Genesis 50, we see that Joseph had years earlier been sold into slavery by his brothers. Then the tables were turned. Joseph had become the governor of all Egypt, and his brothers stood before him, expecting—justifiably—to be condemned by him. But listen to what Joseph said to them: "Do not be afraid, for am I in the place of God?...you meant evil against me, but God meant it for good...."

So it is with you and me. Every occurrence in your life has happened because God either wanted it to happen or allowed it to happen. If someone has hurt you in the past, there is only one attitude that can enable healing in your life: "Whether you did so intentionally, or irresponsibly, or accidentally, you've hurt me in the past, but God is using even that for His good."

Paul, in Philippians 3:13-14, wrote, "One thing I do, forgetting those things which are behind and reaching forward to those things which are ahead, I press toward the goal for the prize of the upward call of God in Christ Jesus." The New Testament emphasizes the fact that the past is done with; our sins are forgiven, forgotten, buried in the deepest sea, remembered no more. Today, we are responsible for today.

There is a priest in the Philippines who had a woman in his parish who deeply loved God. In fact, this woman claimed that at night she often had visions in which she talked with Jesus Christ, and He talked to her. The priest, however, was skeptical of her claims, so to test her visions he said to her, "You say that you actually speak directly with

Christ in your visions. Then, let me ask a favor. The next time you have one of these visions, I want you to ask Him what sin your priest committed when he was in seminary."

The sin the priest spoke of was something he had done in secret, and no one knew except him and Christ. In fact, this years-old sin was a great burden of guilt from which he had been unable to free himself. He wanted forgiveness, but felt he could never be forgiven.

The woman agreed to ask the priest's question in her next vision and went home. When she returned to the church a few days later, the priest said, "Well, did Christ visit you in your dreams?"

"Yes, He did," replied the woman.

"And did you ask Him what sin I committed in seminary?" he asked.

"Yes, I asked Him."

"Well, what did He say?"

"He said, 'I don't remember.' "

If you are a follower of Jesus Christ right now, if you have confessed your sins and turned from them (as the priest did), then that is what He wants you to know about your past: He doesn't remember. The past is over. The sin is forgotten. Today, we are responsible for today.

Not long ago I was counseling a woman who was coming to understand this fact, and she was finding healing and wholeness in her self-image and her emotions. In her past, she had been involved in a long succession of affairs with different men. But all of that was dramatically changed as she had recently come to know the Lord in a personal way. "I've just discovered something wonderful about myself," she told me. "I just realized that today, in God's sight, I am a virgin."

She is absolutely right. The past—with its sins, hurts, and recriminations—is gone, dead, and buried, to be remembered no more.

4. We must emphasize commitment.

The biblical view of counseling involves an understanding that commitment, not freedom from commitment, is the way to meaning and purpose in life. Tragically, our culture has come to view commitment with suspicion; to many the word *commitment* implies restraint of one's personal freedom and potential for growth.

I have visited with pastors and other Christian counselors who have said that their central goal in working with troubled people is to help free people so that they can "grow as a person," so they can "find themselves." That's not what Jesus wants for you and me. Addressing this very issue, He said, "He who finds his life will lose it, and he who loses his life for My sake will find it" (Matt. 10:39). Jesus is talking here about commitment: whoever is committed to self-actualization will lose himself; whoever makes a commitment of his total self to Jesus Christ will find meaning and purpose in life, and a place in eternity.

Julie was an attractive woman who became romantically involved with a man, became pregnant by him, and was subsequently abandoned by him. Julie suffered under an awesome load of guilt during her pregnancy. Seeking relief from that guilt, she consulted a psychiatrist, who told her that the reason she was feeling guilty was because she had set her moral standards too high. He told her that the only way to free herself of the guilt was to become free from those moral commitments, standards, and restrictions that held back her emotional growth.

Julie took her psychiatrist's advice. It seemed to work for a while. She was able to push her guilt down and out of sight for the remainder of her pregnancy. She gave birth to a beautiful baby boy, and she cherished that baby and loved him more than anything else in the world.

One day, a neighbor stopped by Julie's apartment for a visit. To her horror, she saw Julie with her hand about that baby's throat. The neighbor had prevented Julie from strangling that precious baby to death.

Why? Why would Julie want to kill that beautiful little boy, the child she loved more than anything in all of life?

Julie was referred to a Christian counselor. As he worked with her, she began to see that the reason she had almost killed her most precious possession was unresolved guilt. She was trying to punish herself by taking away the most important and precious thing in her life, believing she could never deserve such a beautiful gift of God as that baby. Julie gradually saw her need of commitment to Jesus Christ. As she felt God's acceptance and unconditional love and grace, she began to be healed of her unresolved guilt. Today, Julie is married to a Christian man, and together they raise that little boy for the Lord.

5. *We must teach and exhibit unconditional love.*

Unconditional love is volitional. It is not a kind of love that is rooted in emotions and feelings; it is an act of the *will*. It is the most powerful force in the world, but it's a power that God is only able to wield through you if you have a growing, dynamic relationship with Jesus Christ in your heart and soul.

When I was in seminary, an elderly pastor once asked me, "Is the church a hospital or an army?" Being the young (and perhaps too-ardent) activist I was in those days, I thought for a very brief moment and then replied with conviction, "The church is an army. We're to go out and fulfill the Great Commission. We're to fight injustice and immorality. We're in cosmic warfare with the principalities and powers and world rulers of this present darkness. No question—we're an army."

I can still hear that elderly pastor say to me, "Well, Ron, what kind of an army is it that leaves its wounded deserted on the battlefield?"

Yes, the church is an army, but it must also be a hospital. Too many of our brothers and sisters have been wounded and left deserted on the battlefield. Tragically, many of them have received their worst wounds, not from the enemy, but from other Christians. If we learn and obediently practice God's unconditional love toward each other, then we will see healing within the body of Jesus Christ.

God wants to use each of us as earthen vessels to bring His healing to brokenhearted people. He wants to use us to minister to troubled people, to show them a new meaning and a new purpose, and to give them a new name. God wants to do this in us today, just as He has done in others throughout history.

God went to a man named Abram, and He gave him a new name: Abraham. And God said, "You will have a new meaning, a new dignity. You will be a father of many nations."

Jesus Christ went to Cephas long before he demonstrated any rocklike qualities, and He said, "You are no longer Cephas. From now on, you will be Peter, the Rock, and upon this rock I shall build My church."

Today, Jesus Christ is still in the business of bringing us into wholeness, of giving us a new name, of making splendid new creations of us. We can join with Jesus, playing a part in His ministry of bringing healing and wholeness to troubled people. I believe God has called each of us, as members of the body of Jesus Christ, to share His ministry. He wants to use us, perhaps not as professional therapists, but certainly as members of the family of faith, surrounding the troubled person in our midst with affirmation, understanding, direction, counsel, and unfailing, unconditional love.

The stage musical "Man of La Mancha" tells the story of Don Quixote, the man who dreamed the impossible dream. The story of Don Quixote was first set down almost four hundred years ago by Miguel de Cervantes, a man who lived a life of suffering, grief, and hardship. Early in his life, Cervantes lost his hand in an accident. He later spent years in slavery and in prison.

Through the centuries, literary scholars have puzzled over Cervantes's enigmatic protagonist, Quixote, the soldier who dreamed the impossible dream, who sought to fight the unbeatable foe. Several literary critics have advanced a theory about Cervantes; they suspect that he had a conversion experience, that he came to know Jesus Christ. Writing during the time of the Spanish Inquisition, Cervantes was not free to express his beliefs openly, so he wrote in parable form a sketch of what it might be like to be a man who would follow Christ.

Cervantes depicted the lovable, idealistic, self-styled knight's encounter with a dirty, broken, suffering woman, her eyes filled with tears. Her name is Aldonza. The song Aldonza sings gives a stabbingly poignant insight into Aldonza's wretched condition: "I was born in a ditch by a mother who left me, naked and cold and too hungry to cry. I never blamed her. I'm sure she left me hoping I'd have the good sense to die, for I am nothing."

A waitress by day, a prostitute by night, Aldonza is subject to every crushing indignity, including the ultimate indignity: rape. Despairing, hopeless, clothed in tattered rags, Aldonza encounters a man named Quixote, who shows her the very first act of kindness in her wretched life. "You are not Aldonza," says Quixote. "I give you a new name. You are my lady Dulcinea."

The curtain falls on this scene, and later rises to show Don Quixote on his deathbed, frail, nearly blind, dying, a man of sorrows, acquainted with grief. A beautiful woman, dressed in satin and lace, comes to his bedside.

Unable to see who has come to kneel at his bedside, Quixote asks, "Who is this?"

"Don't you remember?" says the beautiful woman, her eyes shining with tears. "I am your lady. I am Dulcinea."

And Don Quixote nods his head, closes his eyes, and quietly passes away.

"If anyone is in Christ," wrote the apostle Paul, "he is a new creation; old things have passed away; behold, all things have become new" (2 Cor. 5:17). There are people all around us, and people among us, just like Aldonza—people who believe they are nothing, people who have been wounded, abandoned, victimized, trodden on, forgotten. Jesus has the power to give them new life; we have not only the power but the obligation and the privilege to lead them to new life, to unbind them and set them free. We can love them without conditions, showing them that they don't have to perform to be loved. We can give them a new name, and tell them that, like Dulcinea, they can become new creations.

The greatest, most meaningful challenge we can know in life is to be used by God as His channels, His earthen vessels to bring His wholeness. We can be healing agents of God's creative power.

7. PLEASE STAND BY

The Quiet Ministry of Giving Comfort

Do not be afraid...for I am with you (Jer. 1:8).

The greatest model of love that I've ever known was my father. It's been almost ten years since this godly, loving man, who had been my example and my best friend all my life, died in our home town in Iowa.

I was in Minneapolis at the time. I remember that as I was preparing to fly back to Iowa, many well-meaning Christian friends came to me and said, "This is a time for joy. Your father's funeral should be a celebration of his life, and of the fact that he's united now with Christ in eternity."

Everything they said was true. I knew it.

But somehow those words that were intended to comfort me actually made me feel guilty for the grief I felt. It was as if to suggest—as many Christians are suggesting today—that we should deny the emotional level of our being, that as Christians we should no longer feel the emotions that human beings feel.

To deny our emotions is to deny our humanity; if we are human, we will experience sadness and grief, and we will weep. We cannot deny the emotional level of our humanity and remain faithful to the true biblical witness God gives us in His Word.

Death brings grief, suffering, and the pain of separation. That pain lingers with us. It's not quickly ended.

Often when I'm playing with my children, or listening to their prayers, or just watching them grow, I think of my father, and how wonderful he was with children. How he would have enjoyed his grandchildren! I often find myself wishing Dad could be here. A wish like this is not just a wistful thought, either. It's an ache, it's grief, it's the pain of separation. And at times like those I realize that clichés like "Time heals all wounds" are not only trite and glib, they're absolutely wrong.

We never get over grief fully. Time can lessen grief's intensity and its immediate hold over our emotions. But the pain remains; often it springs forth years later, in a poignant and unexpected rush of emotion. Yet some Christians today would tell you that if you really know Christ, then suffering becomes not suffering, pain becomes not pain. Well, pain *is* pain. Christ is beside us to comfort us, but the pain remains.

Ray Stedman, writing in *Discovery Papers*, the sermon transcripts from Peninsula Bible Church, says,

> Many Christians falsely believe that the Bible calls them to a grin-and-bear-it attitude that even a non-Christian can adopt when there is nothing much he can do about a situation. To listen to some of today's sermons and to read some popular books one would think that Christians are being exhorted to screw on a smile and go around saying, "Hallelujah, hallelujah, I've got cancer!"

If we really care about a friend who is suffering, if we are really sensitive to the needs of a grieving person, then we won't treat that wounded soul with a Band-Aid of superficial answers and pat formulas. If we really wish to minister to that suffering person, we will not glibly quote the Scriptures. There are times to exhort and quote the Bible, but there are also times to refrain from quoting and exhorting. To discern those times is to practice empathy, sensitivity, and mature Christian love toward others.

Suffering and sorrow stab deeper into the human soul than words can reach. A word of consolation or a verse of Scripture may seem like the right medicine, but it could be the wrong time. I want to suggest to you that there is a better way, a more healing way, a more biblical way to minister to your suffering or grieving friend. I want to suggest that you just...stand by.

"Do Something!"

The call I had dreaded for so long finally came one night. At the other end of the line was Nancy. Before she said a word, I knew what her message would be: her fiancé, my friend Dave, had died after a long struggle with a terminal illness. She wanted me to go back to Iowa to speak at Dave's funeral.

Dave had been my neighbor for nearly twenty years. For four years we were debate partners in high school. He was within a few weeks of graduating in the top two percent of his class at George Washington University, and he had received a full scholarship to the University of Iowa to study law. He was twenty-two years old.

I drove the long distance from Minneapolis to Clarinda, Iowa, where I had grown up. As I pulled up at the home where Dave's parents and Nancy, his fiancée, waited, I realized that in spite of my training in pastoral care and counseling I had nothing really comforting to say. Words of encouragement seemed to escape me; I had no articulate speech of peace and consolation. All I could do was weep with them.

All I could do was stand by.

Stand by. Those words have a negative connotation today.

We've all heard about violent crimes committed within view of respectable citizens who do nothing but stand by. You may have gone through the uneasy experience of trying to book a seat on a plane, only to be listed as a standby passenger. Or your television screen suddenly goes blank in the fourth quarter of an NFL game; in dismay you read the words, "PLEASE STAND BY." Or perhaps you've been at the scene of some small household disaster—such as a bowl of oatmeal that fell to the floor and shattered—and your spouse said to you, "Don't just stand by and watch! *Do something!*"

To stand by seems to suggest helplessness, inactivity, or apathy. But I urge you to see the act of standing by in a new light, as a positive form of the ministry of healing and consolation.

Often in the Scriptures we see that God encouraged and emboldened His people with the simple promise, "I am standing by you." When the Lord called Jeremiah to be a prophet, Jeremiah replied, "Lord God, behold, I do not know how to speak, for I am only a youth." But God said to Jeremiah, "Go to everyone I send you to, and say whatever I command you. Don't be afraid of them, for I am with you," standing by (Jer. 1:6-7 author's paraphrase).

In Acts 18 we read that the apostle Paul had come to Corinth to preach to the Jews in the synagogue about Jesus the Messiah. But the Jews had violently opposed and derided Paul, and in anger and discouragement Paul had shaken out his clothes at them and shouted that he was through putting up with them. One night the Lord spoke to Paul in a vision: "Do not be afraid; keep on speaking, do not be silent, for I am with you," standing by (vv. 9-10 author's paraphrase).

In his beautiful, tragic book, *Death Be Not Proud*, John Gunther tells of the agony of having to stand by and watch the suffering of his little son Johnny. He writes:

> During Johnny's long illness, I prayed continually to God.
> Naturally, God was always there. He sat beside us during
> the doctor's consultation, as we waited the long vigils out-
> side the operating room, as we rejoiced in the miracle of a
> brief recovery, as we agonized when hope ebbed away and
> the doctors confessed there was no longer anything they
> could do. They were helpless and we were helpless. But God
> in His infinite wisdom, God in His mercy and loving kind-
> ness, God in all of His omnipotence in our hour of need, was
> standing by us.

One of the most insightful Christian writers of our time is
Joe Bayly. He is a man acquainted with grief, having lost
three children—two as teen-agers and one as a five-year-old
child. So Joe Bayly speaks authoritatively as he writes,

> Don't try to prove anything to a survivor. An arm about
> the shoulder, a firm grip of the hand, a kiss: these are the
> proofs that grief needs, not logical reasoning.

He goes on to talk about his experience of grief following the
loss of his third child:

> I was sitting, torn by grief. Someone came and talked to
> me of God's dealings, of why it happened, of hope beyond
> the grave. He talked constantly, he said things I knew were
> true. I was unmoved, except to wish he'd go away. He finally
> did.
> And then another man came and sat beside me for an
> hour or more, listened when I said something, answered
> briefly, prayed simply, left. I was moved. I was comforted. I
> hated to see him go.

God's Surrogate

The crucial fact for us to grasp about the ministry of stand-ing by is this: God wants us to know that He is standing by us. He often chooses to stand by us in the form of another person, a surrogate, a representative.

This principle is illustrated in the example of Jesus Christ Himself. Do you think Jesus ever needed someone to stand by Him? Yes, He did. It was at the hour of His death on the cross, and the person God the Father chose as His represen-tative to His Son was Mary, Jesus' mother. "Now there stood by the cross of Jesus His mother..." the Scriptures tell us in John 19:25.

You may remember that in the story of the crucifixion, the disciples didn't fare very well that day. All the men except John had vanished into the night, but there was Mary, standing by the foot of the cross, representing the love of God to His Son, to her son, to the dying Son of man. Nor was her presence there passive or inactive. When the Gospels mention the presence of the other people who stood by the cross that day, they say that "the people stood looking on" (Luke 23:35). The Roman centurion "stood there in front of Jesus," and the other soldiers, "sitting down,...kept watch over Him" (Matt. 27:36). They stood around the cross, just waiting for Him to die. But the Greek word describing Mary's presence in John 19:25—a word translated "standing by" in English—literally means "to be creatively and compassionately present." Mary ministered to her dying son by her very presence.

Doesn't this suggest a ministry that is within the grasp of us all? Not everyone can be a teacher or a choir director or a theologian. Not everyone can speak prophetically or lead some courageous crusade for the betterment of humankind. But everyone, every follower of Jesus Christ, can perform the ministry of standing by, of being creatively, compassionately present.

What Are We Afraid Of?

Why then do we hold back from standing by a suffering or grieving person? Is it because we're afraid? Are we fearful of sharing the sorrow of that person, ashamed of the tears that might come to our own eyes? Or are we afraid we won't know what to say, that we won't have any words of comfort to give? There's no record in Scripture that Mary, at the cross of Jesus, said anything.

The ministry of standing by often touches far deeper than words. In fact, words in a time of sorrow, pain, or grief can often do more harm than good. Job's so-called comforters came with plenty of words, pious words, judging words. Job's friends had come to interpret Job's troubles to him, to suggest that his suffering was a result of his defection from God, his sin, his loss of faith. We all know how much those words meant to Job in his suffering: They were worse than nothing; they compounded his misery.

Or consider the suffering of Jesus as He prayed in the Garden of Gethsemane. Before Him stood the cross, and the weight of the world's sin. His agony was so great that He sweat drops of blood. Yet after He prayed, He found His closest friends, Peter, James, and John, asleep. Jesus was grieved and He reprimanded them, but not because they didn't stay awake and talk with Him, not because they didn't give Him any words of comfort. What broke the Lord's heart was that they could not watch with Him for even one hour; He was grieved that His friends were sleeping instead of standing by Him.

It's an indictment of us all, that we really seem unwilling as Christians to stick with people in need. In our efforts to win others to Jesus Christ, we are often more willing to coerce people into the kingdom of God than to love them into the Kingdom by simply standing by them. We're willing to spend thousands of dollars on elaborate media evangelism campaigns. We're willing to put on a bumper sticker or a button, or to hand someone a Christian tract. But as an investment of time in human lives, in human souls, these things cost almost nothing. Why are we unwilling to pour a little bit of ourselves into other people, to live sacrificially as our Lord commanded, to be present with people in need?

What I am saying here is not easy. It goes against the grain of our culture, of our pragmatic use of time, of our American values of stoic self-reliance. And it involves sacrifice. It involves pain to stand by someone. It involves inconvenience and lost sleep and time spent in prayer to lay down your life for someone, to stand by someone.

You see, you can't lead somebody out of the desert without going into the desert yourself. You can't have a ministry to hurting people without hurting with them yourself. The essence of a caring community of believers—imitators of Jesus Christ—is this: we've got to lay down our lives for each other, we've got to invest ourselves in each other, we've got to stand by each other.

Three A.M. Christians

Lyman Coleman was meeting with a group of elders, the twenty or so servant-leaders of a large Presbyterian congregation. They were seated in a circle, and Lyman asked this question: "Suppose it's the middle of the night—say, 3:00 o'clock in the morning. You're struggling with an intense problem, you're anxious, troubled, you can't sleep. You can make only one phone call. Who do you call?"

They began to go around the circle. The first elder said he would call a fraternity brother from his college days. The second said he'd call an old friend from his high school football team. The next elder named a boyhood friend from his neighborhood, now living in another town. They went all around the room, and not one of these elders named another of the elders of that church. In fact, no one even named anyone else in the membership of the church.

"I want to suggest to you," said Lyman, "that if there's one place on the face of this earth where that kind of 3 A.M. commitment to each other ought to be taking place, it's right here in the church of Jesus Christ."

One day not long ago, my friend John, who is a college student, came into my office. He was struggling with the Christian faith. He hadn't yet committed his life to Christ, and he had many questions. He was honestly, authentically wrestling within himself, seeking to discover whether the claims of Jesus Christ are real and valid. With tears in his eyes, he told me of an experience he had on his college campus.

As he was eating lunch alone in the cafeteria one day, another young man sat down beside him and struck up a conversation. This new acquaintance seemed to be friendly and outgoing. He appeared to want sincerely to reach out to my friend. That night they went to a movie together, and the next day they went to classes together and then had dinner. For four days this new friend reached out to my friend in every way he could. On the fourth day of their acquaintance, this new friend shared the simple plan of salvation with John.

"I appreciate what you're telling me," John replied, "and to be honest, I've really been doing a lot of thinking about the Christian faith in the past few months. But I'm not to the point of giving my life to Christ yet. I'm still struggling with the decision. I'm just not ready yet."

John said, "You know, Ron, he just got up from the table and I never saw him again the rest of the year."

Perhaps this is a description of you and me, of most of us. Perhaps it's a parable of the church of Jesus Christ today. Maybe you've given up on someone that you need to be standing by. Maybe you don't believe enough in the power of Jesus Christ to redeem an "irredeemable" person. Maybe you don't believe enough in the power of Jesus Christ to heal a broken relationship. Maybe you don't believe enough in the power of Jesus Christ to mend a shattered marriage, and you've counseled your troubled friend to seek a divorce. Perhaps you've lost your own resolve to stand by your mate, and you're headed for divorce yourself.

I want to tell you something that I deeply believe, and I don't say it to lay any kind of judgment or guilt on you. I direct these words to myself first. Like that aggressive four-day evangelist, we may try to minister to someone for awhile, but when we feel we've done our duty, we move on. We walk away.

I have a friend who has toured around the world, witnessing to his Christian faith. One day, during a visit to a poor Third World country, he had a day off from the ministry with which he was involved and he visited a leprosarium. As he was talking with some of the people there who were afflicted with this terrible disease, he met one particular man who had a vital, glowing love for Jesus Christ. The two of them began to visit together.

The leper said to my friend, "You know, I didn't always have this joy, this love of God in my heart. When I first came to this leprosarium I was the most angry and bitter man here.

"But there was one man from the village nearby who came

out every day to visit me. Every single day he came out and brought me food, and at first I threw it back in his face. He'd come out and offer to play cards with me, but I shouted at him to leave me alone. He wanted to talk to me, but I would have nothing to say to him. Still, he kept coming to visit me, day after day after day.

"Finally, I could do nothing else but ask him, 'Why? *Why* do you keep coming to see me, to love me, when all I ever show you is bitterness and hatred?'

"And he told me, 'It's because of the love of Jesus Christ Himself.' "

Then my friend asked the leper, "How long did your friend from the village come out to see you before you gave your heart to Christ?"

The leper's answer: "He came every day for thirteen years."

Does our Christian faith really mean anything? Do we have integrity, and do we have the truth in us when we say we love others? Do we honor the name of Jesus Christ, the name we bear upon ourselves whenever we call ourselves "Christian," by keeping His commandments and following His example? Are we going to talk about love, or are we going to live it? Are we willing to pay the price, to lay down our lives, and to become a fellowship of 3 A.M. Christians? Are we willing to stand by hurting people for as long as it takes?

My prayer is that you will realize that one of the most beautiful gifts you can ever give to another human being—and to Jesus Himself—is the gift of your own life, committed to the sacrifice of self, willing to stand by.

8. A REVOLUTION OF LOVE

God's Unconditional Love Is a Potent Force for Healing

This is how we know what love is: Jesus Christ laid down his life for us. And we ought to lay down our lives for our brothers. . . . Let us not love with words or tongue but with actions and in truth (1 John 3:16,18 NIV).

I want to tell you two stories about two very different kinds of love. It may at first seem ironic, but both of these depictions of love come out of one of the most unloving and unlovely periods of our history—the Vietnam War. I don't believe it's ironic at all, because it is exactly in the most unloving and unlovely times of our lives that a very special kind of love—unconditional love—is so important.

The phone rang in a beautiful suburban home in Boston. The lady of the house answered the phone, heard a pause, then a young man's voice saying, "Hi, Mom." Her son was calling from a phone booth in California. The war in Vietnam was almost over, and he had been sent home from duty in Southeast Asia.

"Son!" she said delightedly. "When are you coming home?!"

"I want to come home right away, Mom. But I wanted to know if it's okay to bring a friend from the service home with me."

"Oh, that's fine, son. We'd love to have one of your friends stay with us for a few days."

"Well, Mom, I think I'd better tell you a little bit about him, first. He may need some extra help. He was badly wounded in Vietnam. He doesn't have a right leg. He doesn't have a right arm. He doesn't have a right eye, and his face is terribly disfigured."

"Well, son," the mother replied, with some hesitancy, "I guess that would be all right—for a few days."

"No, Mom....You still don't quite understand. My friend has nowhere else to go. I want him to live with us. I want him to be part of our family."

There were a few moments of strained silence, and then she said, "Well...I don't think so, son. I'm sorry, but ...you'd better just come alone."

A few hours later, the same phone rang in that Boston home. It was a police sergeant, calling from California. "Ma'am, we have a young man here. Seems he's just back from Vietnam, and he only has one leg, only one arm—and, Ma'am, his identification shows that he's your son. I'm very sorry to have to tell you that your son has just taken his own life."

It was too painful for this young man to ask his mother directly, so he asked indirectly how she would feel about having a physically handicapped person in their home. And tragically, this mother's conditional love seemed to say, "We don't want you at all."

But I have another story to tell you—a story about unconditional love, a love very much like that described in 1 Corinthians 13.

A rubble-strewn village lay still in the aftermath of one of the fiercest battles of the Vietnam War. There were heavy civilian casualties, some of whom were being treated at the badly overcrowded village hospital. Many of the villagers died; of those who survived, most needed blood transfusions. The hospital's supply of whole blood and plasma was soon used up. Everyone in the village donated, some giving more than once. Finally, only one more patient was in critical need of blood. But there was no more blood available to save this man's life.

The doctor went to the orphanage just outside the village to see if one of the children might be willing to give a pint of blood. The doctor stood before the children and asked for volunteers, then waited, but no one volunteered. "No one?" he asked bleakly. "Won't just one of you children give some blood to save a man's life?"

Finally, one hand slipped up in the air, near the back of the room. A twelve-year-old boy volunteered to give his blood.

The doctor took the boy in the next room, told him to lie on a table, inserted the needle in his arm, and proceeded to take blood. As the blood began to flow through the plastic tubing and into the bottle, the boy began to cry openly, profusely. Concerned that this usually painless procedure might be hurting the boy, the doctor stopped the flow of blood.

"Tell me, son," said the doctor, "is this hurting you?"

"No, sir," said the boy. "It doesn't hurt at all."

The blood resumed its flow. The boy continued to cry. Again the doctor shut off the flow of blood into the bottle. "Please, son," said the doctor, "tell me what's the matter."

"Sir," said the boy, "when am I going to die?"

The boy had not understood that his body would soon replace the donated blood; to him, the blood passing through that tube was his very life, draining out of his body. Here is unconditional love, defined in the life of a twelve-year-old Vietnamese boy, who was willing to lay down his life for a man he had never met. Of such an act, Jesus said, "Greater love has no one than this . . ." (John 15:13).

Self-sacrificing, unconditional love is the power of God to mend broken hearts, to give life, to liberate us from fear and guilt and death. Yet most of us have a Grand Canyon in our lives that urgently needs to be bridged: the gulf between human love (conditional love) and God's love (unconditional love), the love of 1 Corinthians 13.

The Most Powerful Force in the World

Our culture is confused about the word *love*. We say that we love pizza; we say we love to go to the beach or to the mountains; we say we love our families; we say we love God. Because this word has come to mean so many different things, it has actually come to mean very little. Love has so many meanings it has no real meaning at all.

But the New Testament Greek word for "love" is a very special word: *agape*. It is different from the Greek word *phileo* (meaning love of family, brotherly love, the instinctive and beautiful love that binds family members together). It is also different from *eros* (meaning the love of attractive, beautiful, pleasing objects such as art or music, or in a similar sense, sexual love and attraction).

When Jesus Christ entered human history, He brought into the world a totally new force, the most powerful force in the world—unconditional love. When Jesus introduced this new love to His disciples, He said, "This is My commandment, that you love one another as I have loved you. Greater love has no one than this, than to lay down one's life for his friends" (John 15:12–13). And that, of course, is exactly what Christ did.

The apostle Paul wrote in Romans 5:8, "God demonstrates His own love toward us, in that while we were still sinners, Christ died for us." God did not extract conditions or promises of good behavior from us; He did not demand that we requite His love to us; He loved us so much that He simply gave His Son to die for us—no conditions asked. That is unconditional love.

When the New Testament was being written, the Greek language had no word for this radical new kind of love. The word *agape*, which occurs repeatedly in the New Testament, can only be found four times in all the rest of classical Greek literature. The early Christians took this obscure and ill-defined word and gave it powerful definition with their very lives—loving each other totally and unconditionally, laying down their time, their possessions, and their lives for each other.

When the time came to write the definition for unconditional love, it was written by the apostle Paul in 1 Corinthians 13. I include it here, and I urge you to read carefully through that beautiful text—even if you know it by heart. As you read, consider the fact that Paul didn't write this chapter to be sentimentalized or idealized. It's not just a sweet-sounding hymn or poem to be read at a bridal shower or a wedding. It's a practical strategy that God wants us to live out, literally and obediently, by the power of the Holy Spirit. It's a practical guide to life in the trenches, for the rough-and-tumble Christian struggle that we face every day of our lives.

Though I speak with the tongues of men and of angels, but have not love, I have become as sounding brass or a clanging cymbal. And though I have the gift of prophecy, and understand all mysteries and all knowledge, and though I have all faith, so that I could remove mountains, but have not love, I am nothing. And though I bestow all my goods to feed the poor, and though I give my body to be burned, but have not love, it profits me nothing. Love suffers long and is kind; love does not envy; love does not parade itself, is not puffed up; does not behave rudely, does not seek its own, is not provoked, thinks no evil; does not rejoice in iniquity, but rejoices in the truth; bears all things, believes all things, hopes all things, endures all things. Love never fails. But whether there are prophecies, they will fail; whether there are tongues, they will cease; whether there is knowledge, it will vanish away. For we know in part and we prophesy in part. But when that which is perfect has come, then that which is in part will be done away. When I was a child, I spoke as a child, I understood as a child, I thought as a child; but when I became a man, I put away childish things. For now we see in a mirror, dimly, but then face to face. Now I know in part, but then I shall know just as I also am known. And now abide faith, hope, love, these three; but the greatest of these is love.

What does Paul say unconditional love is? It's volitional; it's rooted in the will. In fact, it is a self-sacrificing commitment of the will. All other kinds of love, as beautiful as they may be, are essentially instinctive, emotional, temporal, conditional. *Agape* love runs counter to instinct and emotions (to love unconditionally means to love when we don't feel like loving). It is not temporal, but as Paul says, it "always hopes, always perseveres, never fails." It makes no conditions.

The love that most people spend their lives seeking is *eros* love, romantic fulfillment, rooted in feelings and emotion. This love is always temporal, dependent upon emotional highs and conditions of our loved ones' behavior or beauty, or of our image of them. Romantic love seeks to fulfill itself; *agape* love is self-sacrificing.

Agape Love Is Healing Love

Lois was an attractive young Christian woman who took great pride in her physical beauty. She invested much of her self-image and her value as a person in her appearance, in the way she maintained her youthful form through exercise and careful diet, in just the right touch of make-up, in the most fashionable clothes.

One morning as Lois was showering, she noticed a small lump on her breast. She immediately went to her doctor, who sent her to a specialist for a biopsy. The lab report came back: the lump was a malignant tumor. The specialist, a surgeon, performed a mastectomy, the removal of the affected breast. Lois's life was saved, but her self-image and sense of self-worth were shattered.

For six months after that operation, she got up every morning, showered, and dressed, but could not face herself in the mirror. In her heart, she felt that her physical beauty had been cut away from her. How could anyone ever love her now? How could she love herself?

Her emotions in turmoil, Lois sought help from a group of Christians who met weekly to study the Bible, praying for each other, supporting each other. As she met each week with other believers in this house church, she saw that others in the group were struggling with different areas of pain in their lives and were gradually coming into wholeness together. She began to open up about different areas of brokenness in her life, including her fear, worry, depression, anger, and self-hate over her mastectomy. The others in the group demonstrated warmth, love, prayer, and genuine support for Lois, helping her to understand that her worth to God and to other people was in her character, in who she was. They loved her unconditionally and showed her that God does too.

Lois began to be healed in her spirit and her self-image. One day she was able to get out of bed with a prayer of gratitude on her lips, shower, then stand before the mirror and accept herself as she was. Lois had learned to stop thinking like the culture around her, seeking fulfillment in the *eros* kind of love that passes away; she had learned to think and to love like a child of God. She had received unconditional *agape* love, and she was soon able to give this same unfailing, persevering, all-accepting love to herself and to others.

Agape love reaches the most deeply-wounded and unreachable heart. There was a little boy with severe emotional problems. He was a disciplinary problem at home and in school. He received counseling from a psychologist, but nothing seemed to help. He felt rejected, unloved, uncared for, incapable of measuring up to anyone's expectations.

After weeks of vainly trying to find a way to reach the boy, the psychologist called in his parents and said, "One thing you might try is to buy the boy a pet—a little dog, perhaps. He may be able to relate to a puppy."

The parents took the doctor's advice, bought a puppy, and brought him home. When they took their son into the backyard and presented him with the puppy, he made no move toward it, but just stood glaring sullenly.

"Let's leave him alone for awhile," said the father, and they reluctantly went inside.

Soon, the puppy came bounding up to the little boy, wagging its tail, yelping playfully. The boy turned and kicked the dog savagely, as hard as he could. The dog rolled, flailing, into the grass, then scrambled painfully to all fours, eyeing the boy quizzically. The dog hesitated only for a moment, then again came bounding back to his new master, and began to lick the boy's hand lovingly.

The screen door crashed open, and the little boy ran into the living room where his parents waited. "Mom! Dad!" cried the boy, with tears welling in his eyes. "I kicked my puppy, but my puppy still loves me!" At that moment, this broken, angry, withdrawn little boy began to be healed, and the force that started that healing process was a puppy's unconditional love.

What is the trial, the affliction, the suffering that you are undergoing right now? Is it a broken relationship with a friend, a family member, another Christian? Is it an ordeal of having to live with a troubled person, of having to face a commitment to a trouble-plagued marriage? Is it a cloud of gnawing fear or guilt, or deep emotional scars from your past, a recurring sense of worthlessness, self-pity, or even self-hate?

Learning To Love

I want to suggest to you that the prescription for the ultimate healing of broken relationships, broken marriages, broken lives, and broken self-esteem is the unconditional love of Christ and His church.

But how can you learn to love unconditionally, no strings attached? First, you must begin to love God unconditionally. You must love Him, as Deuteronomy 6:5 says, "with all your heart, with all your soul, and with all your might." You must love Him as He is, not as you'd like Him to be. You shouldn't try to change Him or make demands on Him. Instead, bow to His holiness and perfection, and allow Him to change you.

Secondly, you must begin to love yourself unconditionally. That doesn't mean pampering, praising, excusing, worshiping yourself, or fulfilling, "actualizing," indulging, or "looking out for number one," as our culture is always telling us we should. No, it simply means accepting yourself. Know that you have been unconditionally accepted by God's love and grace. God has affirmed your worth by loving you enough to send His Son to die in your place.

We are sinful by nature; we fail and disappoint God, and we disappoint ourselves. Sometimes it seems our sins are so great, so many, that we can never earn God's forgiveness.

And we can't earn it. We can only accept His forgiveness and accept ourselves. Understand that there is no sin so great that God's love and forgiveness isn't greater. Don't excuse yourself. Turn to the Light, ask His forgiveness, and accept yourself as God does. You are unconditionally forgiven, loved, and accepted in Christ.

Next, learn to love others unconditionally. That means both your friends and the difficult people in your life. It means fellow Christians, and it means the arrogant, rude colleague or customer at work. When you apply God's unconditional love to a person who is hurting, grieving, or suffering, then it becomes a potent force for healing and witness to God's life-changing power.

There are two ways to bring a little chick out of an egg and into the world. One way is to hammer away at the egg. You can easily break the shell open, but when the chick emerges it is premature, bruised, and battered. It inevitably dies. How else can you bring that chick out of its shell? You can surround it with warmth, treat it with patience, and protect it from harm (and people with hammers). In God's good time, that shell will crack open, and the chick will come forth alive and whole.

There are a lot of people, many of them in the church, who have been hurt in the past or who are suffering now and who have retreated into protective shells of withdrawal. Many other people—again, many of them in the church—are going about, armed with hammers, determined to help their poor brethren out of their shells, right now, ready or not.

I believe a better way to bring healing to such people is to surround them with an atmosphere of warmth, steadfast patience, and protective care. We can see healing happen by letting unconditional love work, by letting the Holy Spirit minister quietly through us, by letting God bring that person forth in new life, spiritual growth, and emotional wholeness.

When our Rachael, prematurely born and struggling for life, had passed the extreme crisis stage, the doctors encouraged us to put our hands through the cuffs in the incubator and stroke her arms and legs. We learned that even tiny premature babies, only two or three pounds in weight, experienced a noticeably higher survival rate when they regularly experienced this loving, parental touch. Somehow, even the smallest premature baby understands and feels the need of human warmth and love.

I believe we should make a solid commitment in all our relationships with others to see that 90 percent of the things we say and do will be positive and affirmative. I'm not advocating empty praise or insincere flattery; I'm talking here about honestly affirming others, just as God has loved and affirmed us unconditionally. We should seek, for example, to find others' true gifts and to affirm those gifts in Jesus Christ.

A common philosophy today is that you can build someone up by tearing them down. But when you look at it logically—and especially when you look at it biblically, from the perspective of unconditional love—it's clear that this can never happen. Rather, you need to spend the vast majority of your time and energy with others—with your children, with your mate, with your friends, with your Christian brothers and sisters, with that difficult person who is such a struggle in your life—finding ways to build them up, to affirm them, to see the gifts God has given them. Then, and only then, do you have the right and the credibility to challenge them in love when you see sin or error in their lives.

My daughter Rachael is eight years old now, and I have made it a point for the last five years to set aside the lunch hour every Friday just for her. No matter how busy I am, that time is inviolate. I use that time every week for the single purpose of telling her I'm on her team, that I stand with her, that I believe in her, that she is created in the image of God.

Just as Shirley and I used to put our hands into that hospital incubator and stroke her and give her that physical touch of affirmation as she struggled for life, I now make a point of stroking her emotionally, not in a meaningless or disingenuous way, but honestly and lovingly. Then, when I correct her and discipline her, when I have to challenge the way she is behaving, it occurs in an atmosphere where the preponderance of our relationship has been warm, affirmative, constructive, and unconditionally loving.

Look Past the Irritation

Who are you struggling with today? What person is causing you anger, annoyance, heartache, or irritation? There is a phrase that has been helpful for me to recall in my dealings with difficult or troubled people—young people coming off drugs, who are often very hard to love; people who oppose my ministry; people I try to help in counseling settings who are looking to place blame and who sometimes strike out at me. The phrase is simply this: *Look past the irritation to the need.* This, I think, is part of the essence of the gospel; it is unconditional love expressed in a nutshell.

When the relationship with a family member, a coworker, or someone in your church is strained and challenged, learn to look past the irritation he or she causes you and begin to see the need in that person's life. Does this apply to those who go out of their way to hurt us, the people who actually seem to hate us and take pleasure in offending us? Yes, it especially applies to such situations.

Look closely at the brash, arrogant, self-important person, and you'll often see a person who is deeply insecure, unsure of his or her self-worth, constantly needing to reassure and build himself or herself up at the expense of others. Look closely at the quarrelsome person who constantly contends and debates with you, and you may see someone who is confused underneath it all, someone who seeks to be convinced that your Christian witness is true. Look closely at the person who is sullen and withdrawn and hostile, and you'll often find someone who has been deeply wounded in mind and spirit since childhood, someone who is desperate to be loved without conditions, without having to measure up to someone else's expectations.

Look past the irritation to the need in that person's life. See him or her as someone for whom Christ gave Himself, and give yourself in the same way. I believe that if you do, in most cases you will see healing.

What is your trial right now? Is it a rumor being circulated about you, damaging your reputation and hurting your relationships with friends and coworkers? How are you responding? Our natural inclination is to strike out, to get even, to become bitter and resentful. We say, "It's not fair! It's not right! I don't deserve to be treated this way."

There's an East Coast halfway house for troubled people, with this motto hanging over the front door: "Do you want to be right, or well?" You can't always have it both ways. When someone spreads a false report about us, we often try so hard to justify ourselves that we become spiritually and emotionally ill. It's a well-documented fact that emotional ills can help bring on physical ailments as well. If we want to find completeness and wholeness in Jesus Christ, then we may have to give up the dubious luxury of always being right.

What should our response be when we are hurt by a rumor? First, set aside self-pity and resentment, because you are justified by faith in Jesus Christ; He has justified you, so you've no need to justify yourself. Second, understand that if you must patiently withstand an evil report, even a report that has wrongly been spread by another Christian, then you will find favor with God.

"For this is commendable," says 1 Peter 2:19–20, "if because of conscience toward God one endures grief, suffering wrongfully.... When you do good and suffer for it, if you take it patiently, this is commendable before God." Why? Because Jesus Himself suffered and was reviled for us, though He did no wrong. Patiently suffering from unjust rumors is an act of conformity to the image of Jesus Christ, and it is a positive act of unconditional love.

The Only Love Worthy of the Name

Tommy was a college student. One of his teachers, John Powell, was a Christian. John had taken many opportunities to talk to Tommy, and he knew him to be a hardened atheist, an angry young man who had rejected God, parents, and society. His relationship with his family was totally broken. John repeatedly tried to reach Tommy, to witness to him, to love him unconditionally. But there seemed to be no change in Tommy's heart.

Eventually Tommy graduated. He walked out of the classroom and out of reach forever—or so John Powell thought.

Some time later, John was working at his desk after classes. The classroom door opened, and John looked up to see Tommy standing in the doorway. At first, John didn't recognize him; he had changed. He looked frail and wasted; the long hair he had previously worn as a symbol of rebellion was entirely gone. Though his eyes were bright and his voice firm, it was clear to John Powell that the young man who stood before him had been ravaged by cancer and the effects of chemotherapy.

Tommy sat down and began to talk to his former teacher. Gone were the anger and arrogance of his days at school. It was replaced by a calm self-assurance that John had never before seen in Tommy.

"When the doctors found a malignant tumor in my groin," said Tommy, "I began to get serious about trying to find God. And when they told me that the cancer had spread into my vital organs, I really began to beat my fists against the doors of heaven. I couldn't understand why God was silent, why He wouldn't come out. I was alone and I knew I was going to die. So I decided to spend the time I had left doing something profitable.

"I thought about the talks you and I had. I remembered something you said: 'One of the saddest things in the world is to go through life without ever knowing how to love unconditionally. But it may be even more sad to go through life and leave this world without ever telling the people you care about that you love them.'

"Mr. Powell, I finally saw what you meant. And even though it came to me late in my short life, I decided to begin to love as you said, and to tell people I love them. And I decided to begin with the hardest case. You know who I mean: my dad.

"I went to my parents' house. My dad was reading the paper. I said, 'Dad?' and he said, 'What?' and that newspaper didn't even rustle. I said, 'Dad, I really want to talk to you.' He said, 'Well, talk.' I said, 'Dad, it's really important.' He lowered that newspaper a couple of inches and glanced across at me; he was annoyed, and he didn't want to be bothered. It wasn't exactly the way I had pictured it would be, and it was the hardest thing I've ever done in my life, but

I looked him in the eye and said, 'Dad, I love you. I just wanted you to know that. I really love you.' "

Tommy smiled as though he felt a warm and secret joy inside him. "My dad dropped that newspaper like he'd been hit in the chest. Then he did two things I can never remember him doing before: he cried and he hugged me. We talked all night, even though he had to go to work the next morning.

"It was easier with my mother and my little brother. They cried with me too, and we hugged each other and shared things we had been keeping secret for years. I only regretted one thing: that I had waited so long. I waited until almost the very end of my life to open up to the people I had really loved all my life.

"Not long after this, I turned around and suddenly realized that God was there. I talked to Him, felt His love and acceptance and forgiveness, and received Christ as my Lord and Savior. While I was learning about His unconditional love, it was penetrating into my heart."

My friend asked Tommy if he would be willing to share this story with his classes. Tommy said that he would; it was something he wanted to do both for John and for Jesus Christ. They scheduled a date, but Tommy never made it. He had another appointment to keep.

Shortly before he died, Tommy called John Powell one last time. "I'm not going to make it to your class," he said.

"I know," said John.

"Well, will you tell them for me, Mr. Powell?"

"I will, Tommy. I'll tell them."

What Tommy wanted my friend to tell his students was that unconditional love is the only way to know God, the only way to become conformed to the image of Christ, the only way to become whole and to triumph over tragedy. The only love worthy of its name is unconditional love, rooted in a personal relationship with Jesus Christ.

Unconditional love can bring healing to broken relationships, as it did with Tommy and his father. It can bring healing to people who are troubled in mind, spirit, and emotions, as it did in the lives of Lois and the troubled little boy. It can even bring wholeness in the midst of unspeakable tragedy and the shadow of death, as in Tommy's life and death.

Unconditional love is not just the answer to our problems and sufferings; it is greater than our problems and sufferings! It may be that we will be called on by God to love someone unconditionally for months or years and still see no results in that person's life. We may never see that person's heart soften, his life yielded to God, or his hostility transformed to love. Ultimately, results are not our business but God's.

Unconditional love is not a tool to be manipulated for our own ends; it's the power of God's will. It is what He has commanded us to do. Our part is not to evaluate results but to do His will obediently.

One thing is guaranteed: if we practice this kind of love, we will find healing and wholeness in our lives. And we'll find power to live a life patterned after the image of Jesus Christ. That is, after all, God's ultimate goal for each of us.

Unconditional love is the most powerful force in the world. It's the only love worthy of the name.

9. NEVER ALONE

Biblical Counsel for Loneliness

And the LORD, He is the one who goes before you. He will be with you, He will not leave you nor forsake you; do not fear nor be dismayed (Deut. 31:8).

Keith Miller, in his book *Living The Adventure*, relates this letter from a woman named Alice, who knows very well what loneliness means:

When I was a little girl, I was put in an orphanage. I wasn't pretty at all, and no one wanted me. But I can recall longing to be adopted and loved by a family as far back as I can remember. I thought about it day and night. But everything I did seemed to go wrong. I always tried too hard to please everybody who came to look me over, and all I did was drive people away.

Then one day the head of the orphanage told me a family was going to take me home with them. I was so excited, I jumped up and down and cried. The matron reminded me that I was on trial and that it might not be a permanent arrangement. But I just knew it would be.

So I went with this family and started to school in their town, a very happy girl. And life began to open for me, just a little.

One day, a few months later, I skipped home from school and ran in the front door of the house. No one was home, but there in the middle of the front hall was my battered old suitcase with my coat thrown over it. As I stood there and looked at that suitcase, it slowly dawned on me what it meant: They didn't want me—and I hadn't even suspected.

That happened to me seven times before I was thirteen years old.

Now an adult, Alice has spent months in counseling, struggling to understand and overcome her deep emotional scars of rejection and loneliness.

Loneliness has been called "the most desolate word in the world." We've all felt the truth of that statement at one time or another. Perhaps your life is a desolate, lonely place even now. You may be wondering, "When will this pain end? How can anyone survive such loneliness?"

I don't claim to have a cure for loneliness. I don't believe an instant solution to such profound emotional longings exists. But I believe the Bible offers a response that will enable you to survive your lonely condition and to obtain a resounding spiritual victory through it all. I believe there is a plan that Jesus Christ wants to work out in your life through your present feelings of isolation and despair.

Most of all, I believe He wants you to know that you're never truly alone.

Grief and Loneliness

A friend of mine, a widow, spent thirty years married to one man. One day her deeply loving, Christian husband suddenly succumbed to a heart attack, and she was alone. That was several years ago, and ever since then her life has been a succession of lonely, joyless days. At one time, she told me that I could never fully understand the ache of her life. I knew she was right.

"You have no idea what it's like," she said, "to come home

every day, to fix a meal for one, to set the table for one, to wash the dishes for one, and to look across the table night after night at the chair once occupied by my husband. When someone tells me time will heal it all, I get angry! Time hasn't healed my pain. Not a bit." My friend is right. There's not enough time in the world to completely heal such a wound.

After the death of his mother, author Henri Nouwen wrote these words to his grieving father:

> Real grief is not healed by time. It is false to think that the passing of time will slowly make us forget her and take away our pain. I really want to console you in this letter, but not by suggesting that time will take away your pain, and that in one, two or three more years you will not miss her anymore. I would not only be telling a lie, I would be diminishing the importance of mother's life and underestimating the depth of your love for her, shared together for 47 years. If time does anything, it deepens our grief. The longer we live, the more fully we become aware of who she was for us, and the more intimately we experience what her love meant for us (from *A Letter of Consolation*).

Listen to the words of another letter shared with me recently. The letter was written by a young woman who had been deeply in love with a young man, and had become engaged to marry him. Suddenly he had broken their engagement and had left her for another. Now she was leaving her church and community, and going back to her home town to live with her parents. "I can't stay here anymore," she wrote. "Neither a good job nor a sound, friendly church like ours can remove the long, lonely ache from my heart. I'm going back home now more lonely than I ever dreamed possible."

Loneliness touches us all. It afflicts the divorcée, the family that has lost a little child, the older people who have become separated from loved ones by loss or distance, the student who is away from home for the first time.

Loneliness and the Believer

"What a Friend we have in Jesus," we sing. Though it's a profound and comforting truth, we must be honest and confess that loneliness touches the follower of Christ as well as those who have no hope in Him.

One man, a Christian lay leader, strong in his witness for Christ, came to know loneliness intimately and tragically. Over a period of time, he gradually lost his health, then his job, then his wife, and finally he lost the greatest joy of his life, next to Christ—he lost his little son in a tragic accident. He was alone.

In his grief, all he had to turn to was his photo albums. One day, he took the photos of his son and covered one huge wall of his house, ceiling to floor, with them. And that evening he took his own life.

Loneliness knows no barrier. It invades all of our lives at one time or another.

The Ministry of Interruptions

Tears streamed down the face of my seminary professor as he told me a story from his days in the pastorate. In those days, he had been the pastor of a large midwestern church. He was an effective preacher, a gifted evangelist. He was also a very disciplined man, a great believer in time management.

One day, a layman named Mr. Harrison came into the church office and stopped before the secretary's desk. "Excuse me," he said. "I'd like to speak to the pastor."

The secretary hesitated. "I'm sorry. Today is the pastor's

day for study and sermon preparation. But if you'd like to make an appointment—"

"It won't wait," said Mr. Harrison. "Please—if I could just see the pastor for a few moments."

The secretary could see that Mr. Harrison was in need—lonely and depressed. "Just a moment," she said. "I'll ask if he can see you now."

She went into this pastor's study and told him about Mr. Harrison. "If you could just see him for a few moments—"

The pastor said, "You know this is the only time I have for sermon preparation. Tell Mr. Harrison I can see him next Wednesday, 3 P.M."

"But I think he really needs—"

"*Wednesday.*"

The secretary went out and told him, "Pastor can see you at 3 P.M., next Wednesday."

Mr. Harrison sighed. "All right. Thank you." Despondently, he turned, walked out of that church, went home, and shot himself to death.

"I know God has forgiven me," concluded that pastor —my professor—as he wiped the tears from his eyes. "But I have never been able to forgive myself."

One of the most basic and fruitful ministries you and I can have is the one form of ministry we are usually least open to. I call it *the ministry of interruptions.*

God wants us to understand that the interruptions that come into our well-ordered lives have a purpose. He wants us to see that Mr. Harrison is the only one who counts. He is the one for whom we are willing to discard our daily schedules, our cherished plans, our vital responsibilities, our meetings and luncheons—not because they're not important, but because they lose their consuming sense of urgency in light of the true urgency of Mr. Harrison's need. He matters. He is the one lost sheep that the Good Shepherd laid down His life to find and save.

Ruth Harmes Cauken, in her book *Lord, You Love To Say Yes*, tells about the day she carefully planned her spiritual retreat alone with God. She set aside her busy schedule, took her Bible and notebook, and prepared to spend the day in study, meditation, and intercessory prayer.

Within a few minutes, the phone rang. She hurried through a conversation with a chatty neighbor, then returned to her Bible and notebook. Then there was another call. And another, and another. Her husband came home sick from work, so she had to spend more time on the phone, canceling his appointments. The mail brought not one, but two disturbing letters. A cousin, whose name she couldn't even recall, happened to stop by on her way through town.

"And yet," she concludes, "dear Lord, You were with me in it all....Perhaps in Your great wisdom and grace, You longed to teach me a practical truth: When You are my spiritual retreat, I need not be a spiritual recluse." This is a lesson we all need to learn.

The Loneliest Time of Year

I've found there is one time of year when awareness of the ministry of interruptions is more crucial than at any other time. Statistically, it is a time when there is more alcohol abuse, more drug abuse, more hospitalization, more emotional trauma, more suicide and attempted suicide—that is, more loneliness—than at any other time of the year.

The loneliest time of the year is Christmas.

One Christmas season, not long ago, I received a letter from a friend of our family—the kind of letter I receive all too often. She was undergoing a trial of separation and divorce during the holiday season. She closed by writing, "I feel terribly alone. I have been hurt and humiliated. I have no reason to live anymore."

For many of us, the holidays are no holiday at all. Often, Christmas is a bittersweet time, a time when fond memories of past holiday seasons and lost loved ones actually deepen our loneliness and depression. Nostalgic remembrances of family Christmases before the divorce, or of the plans made with that ex-fiancée, who is now married to another—these remembrances bring a kind of pain at Christmas that occurs at no other time during the year. For many, and perhaps for you, Christmas serves only as a stark reminder of loneliness and loss.

For others, Christmas is not a lonely time, but a busy time. There are presents to buy, gifts to wrap, cards to mail, letters to write, food to buy, calls to make, family gatherings to plan, parties to attend, too much traffic, too much work, not enough time—for interruptions.

Not enough time for the lonely, desperate, hurting interruptions, like Mr. Harrison.

The ministry of interruptions is a ministry of sensitivity to others and to the Holy Spirit; of openness; of sharing; of caring; of taking the time to allow ourselves to be interrupted for Jesus' sake, even during the loneliest, busiest, and—if we dare to be so vulnerable—potentially the most crucial time of year.

After all, this is what Christmas is really about: the birth of the One who came to save those who are lost and lonely and dying. May God give us the sensitivity and awareness to see the Mr. Harrisons around us, the insight to recognize them as opportunities instead of intrusions, and the boldness and unconditional love to reach out to them.

People Who Laugh and Cry

In her book *Mourning Song* Joyce Landorf tells the story her father told her shortly after her mother's death. The event he told about happened when her father was only eight years old.

One day as he was at school, his aunt came early to take him home. On the way home, the boy asked, "Why did I have to leave school?"

Abruptly, sternly, without any emotion, his aunt replied, "Your father is dead."

The cruel weight of these unsympathetic words began to crush this young boy as they rode home in silence. Tears began to pour down his face.

The aunt, noticing the tears, suddenly struck the boy's face and commanded, "Don't you dare cry!"

"Those moments, so long past," Joyce Landorf concludes, "were the moments when my daddy shut off his feelings and emotions, and they would live buried deep inside him for the rest of his life."

In not as harsh or dramatic a way, but in ways just as real, you may have shut off some of those emotions too. Perhaps you are lonely because you are unwilling to share your life with the ones around you who are ready to love you. Maybe that wall of loneliness around your heart is one that has been erected there by some past trauma, some deep emotional scar. You need to open your feelings to others, to share your tears.

God has made us with a mind, and with that mind we are to reach our ultimate potential. He has made us with a will, and with that will we are to reach our ultimate obedience. He has made us with emotion, and with that emotion we are to reach our ultimate openness in relationship with Him and with others.

I go back again and again to the words of C. S. Lewis, "Christians are people who laugh and cry a lot." I recently had an experience, during a church conference in the Midwest, of meeting some wonderful new Christian friends—laughing with them, praising the Lord with them, enjoying their company, singing with them, and experiencing great joy. Later that evening I was relaxing at the home of one of the couples in that church, good friends of mine, and we were sharing together. Suddenly, nostalgically, they began to share about the birth and death of their little baby four years ago. Tears came to our eyes as Dave, the father, shared that he is still unable to sit through a baptism without having to excuse himself as the tears stream down his face. Yes, Christians are people who laugh—and cry—a lot.

If it's any help to you, my life at times is filled with deep feelings of sorrow. There are times when my depression or grief or hurt is so intense that I actually cry aloud to God; those experiences usually come when I'm alone, driving in the car, out running, or lying in bed at night.

I've cried aloud to God at times when I've recalled a sobering, heartbreaking trip I recently took with three friends to Kenya, Africa, where World Vision is caring for desperately sick and hungry people. I think of the little babies we held in our arms, babies so badly malnourished that the doctors said they had little chance of living more than a few days or weeks. I remember holding those babies, and I grieve over the fact that, despite the best efforts of World Vision's skilled doctors and nurses, many of them have died needlessly by now of malnutrition or a simple childhood disease like measles.

I cry aloud to God when I think of friends, close friends, intimate friends, who are moving to a distant city; I feel the pain of that impending separation keenly, and I grieve even during the time before they're gone.

Sometimes, grief stabs at me during the happiest times. I'll be playing with my children, enjoying their laughter and playfulness, and suddenly the thought comes to me that my dad would really have enjoyed his grandchildren. But he never knew his grandchildren, and I miss him and keenly feel that loss to this day.

There are other times when, in disillusionment, I lift my hands to the Father and tell Him aloud about my deepest feelings and struggles.

I really believe these are no different from the feelings expressed in many places in Scripture. For example, look at Psalm 22, a psalm of despondent questioning in the face of suffering and loneliness. Verse 1: "My God, My God, why have You forsaken Me?/Why are You so far from helping Me,/And from the words of My groaning?" Verse 11: "Be not far from Me,/For trouble is near;/For there is none to help."

This is a psalm of David, and a psalm of the suffering Messiah, Jesus Christ. But it is also your psalm, when you feel forsaken, rejected, oppressed, lonely. Why? Because it doesn't end in despair, but with words such as these:

> "You have answered Me.
> I will declare Your name to My brethren;
> In the midst of the congregation I will praise You.
> . . . He has not despised nor abhorred
>   the affliction of the afflicted;
> Nor has He hidden His face from Him;
> But when He cried to Him, He heard" (vv. 21–22,24).

God is equally moved with both our expressions of sorrow and our expressions of joyful praise: He weeps with us as we weep and rejoices with our joy. He is touched with the feel-

ings of our lives—our joy, our sorrow, our doubt, our loneliness—just as He is touched with the feelings of the psalmist.

Paul, the Lonely Apostle

Have you ever considered, as you've studied Acts and the
Epistles, what a lonely man the apostle Paul must have been?
I think it's important, as we try to understand a passage of
Scripture, that we consider the circumstances of the people
involved. I believe one of the most crucial and ever-present
circumstances in Paul's life was loneliness. Let me list a few
reasons.

First, Paul was once married, and—either because his wife
had died or left him after his conversion—he no longer enjoyed her companionship. There's no place in Scripture that
flatly states that Paul was ever married. However, we do
know that the preconversion Paul was a rabbi (see, for example, Phil. 3). According to Jewish tradition, a man who did
not marry was said to have slain his posterity. Rabbinic
tradition also held that there were seven who would be ex-
communicated from heaven, and the first of these was a Jew
who had not married. Moreover, it was required that all of
the Sanhedrin—of which Paul was a member (see Acts
26:10)—be married, because it was thought that married
men would be more merciful than unmarried men.

It is unthinkable in my view that the preconversion Paul,
the rabbi and Sanhedrin council-member, would have been
unmarried. Accordingly, I think it's clear that the postcon-
version Paul, who no longer shared the companionship of a
wife, must have been lonely.

Second, I believe Paul was lonely because he was often imprisoned. One historian, after seeing for himself the Roman
prison where Paul was confined, wrote about "the dismal,
dark, low-arched chamber where the apostle once lay

bound, waiting to be offered up. Even on a hot summer day, the visitor in Rome will sense the constriction of the low ceiling and the dampness of the dark dungeon." Paul spent much of his life in such places.

Third, I believe Paul was lonely because he often had no traveling companions. We see in his life and letters that Paul was committed to being together with others in ministry. Yet we also see, due to the hard realities of first century travel and his frequent imprisonment, Paul was often alone in his travels.

In 2 Timothy 4:9-16, Paul was writing to Timothy, pleading with him to come to him soon, because "Demas has forsaken me, having loved this present world, and has departed for Thessalonica—Crescens for Galatia, Titus for Dalmatia. Only Luke is with me. . . . Tychicus I have sent to Ephesus. . . . Alexander the coppersmith did me much harm. . . . At my first defense no one stood with me, but all forsook me." How clear and poignant is the message between these lines: Paul had been forsaken by some and left by others for the sake of the gospel. His spiritual son, Timothy, was miles away. Paul was lonely.

Fourth, Paul experienced the special pain and loneliness of being deserted by his Christian friends, his own beloved brothers in the faith. We see this fact in the passage just quoted from 2 Timothy. We also see it in other passages, such as Galatians 1. There is a sense of wounded, stunned amazement in Paul's letter—amazement at how quickly the Galatians had questioned his apostleship and his leadership, and had turned from their new-found faith. "I marvel," he wrote, "that you are turning away so soon from Him who called you in the grace of Christ, to a different gospel." How lonely Paul must have felt to see the spiritual defection of his Galatian friends.

Fifth, Paul was lonely because he was constantly stalked by

death. In fact, Paul seemed to have a constant sense of death throughout his Christian life. "To live is Christ, and to die is gain," he wrote in Philippians 1:21. In 2 Timothy 4:6–7, "The time of my departure is at hand. I have fought the good fight, I have finished the race, I have kept the faith."

These and other passages of Paul's display a courageous spirit; but they also depict a lonely spirit. Paul faced what we all know (though we often refuse to face it): Each of us must face the last enemy, death, alone. Surely we have Christ alongside us, but no other human being can walk the pathway to eternity with us. It is a lonely path.

Loneliness Transformed

How did Paul respond to the loneliness that pervaded his life? Did he succumb to it? Did it paralyze him? Did it hinder his ministry? No, throughout his letters, throughout Luke's account of his life in Acts, we sense a note of challenge, victory, and adventure in Paul's often hard and lonely life. How is this possible? How could Paul survive his loneliness without its robbing him of his joy and will to live?

How can anyone survive loneliness?

I believe we can discover three principles in the life of Paul, three specific actions he took, in his personal, spiritual struggle against loneliness.

First, Paul sought out the companionship and fellowship of Christian brothers. He took the initiative. He had many partners in ministry: Timothy, Barnabas, Luke, Tychicus, Titus, Epaphras.

When you are lonely, when you feel the tendrils of depression start to close in around your spirit, you need to take the initiative toward companionship and fellowship with specifically chosen, godly people. Loneliness is fed by isolation. If no one reaches out to you, then you must reach out.

You have to become open enough and vulnerable enough to admit your own weakness, your own humanness to others. Find those selected people with whom you can share yourself and say, "You know, I'm having a tough time right now. I'm lonely. I need your friendship."

Why are we unable to do that? Because our culture teaches us that it's a sign of weakness. So what? We *are* weak! And if we can have the courage to admit our weakness, then we can become more like Christ, and we can liberate ourselves from enslavement to loneliness and depression. I believe you will find that by taking that one courageous step, you will liberate your new friend to share his or her own weakness, loneliness, and brokenness.

The second action Paul took against loneliness was that he let himself *be* himself. He had the courage and integrity to live out his beliefs. He did not vacillate according to popular opinion. He was not a people-pleaser; he was a God-pleaser. "We speak, not as pleasing men," wrote Paul, "but God who tests our hearts" (1 Thess. 2:4).

I was nineteen years old, preaching in a small rural church in the Midwest. I noticed that one of the elders of that church, a particularly strong-willed man, had just entered the sanctuary. From past experience with him, I knew that there was one point in my prepared sermon that he would disagree with. I wanted his approval, so I omitted that point. I compromised the message God had given me, and I compromised my integrity. I became a people-pleaser.

The problem with living this way is that it never makes you less alone. It only compounds your guilt. God calls us to freedom from having to please others, freedom from guilt. He calls us to make our central aim in life to please Him. "Do I seek to please men?" asked Paul. "For if I still pleased men, I would not be a servant of Christ" (Gal. 1:10). Notice Paul's principle: If I am a people-pleaser, I cannot be a Christ-servant.

Third, Paul realized that only a cause greater than himself could rid him of his loneliness. We see that Paul was lonely, but we never see him wrapped up in his own concerns, never wallowing in self-pity. His eyes were set on a cause and a goal that transcended his own condition.

How many times have we heard someone say, "I've got to get myself together, then I'll be able to serve God." Or, "I've got to find myself, get into myself, discover who I am and who I want to become."

Jesus says to us, "Give yourself away to others. Find a cause that is greater than yourself. Find the greatest cause in the world. Come, and follow Me." The way to fulfillment, peace, and wholeness is not inward but outward, in service to others and to Jesus Christ. "He who finds his life will lose it, and he who loses his life for My sake will find it," says Christ (Matt. 10:39).

Dr. Thomas Malone, a noted Christian psychologist, has said that the people he has counseled fall essentially into two groups. The first group is composed of lonely, broken people who desperately cry, "Please love me." The second group is composed of people who hurt, but are whole enough to demonstrate love and caring for the people in the first group. Interestingly, the most therapeutic way these people can respond to their loneliness is for them to take the risk of becoming open and caring toward the people in the first group. If they become willing to reach out and serve others, says Dr. Malone, they will automatically begin to fill the void of self-worth, self-esteem, and love within themselves.

Who can understand the fear and loneliness of someone with a terminal illness? Who understands the heartache of divorce and separation? Who can comprehend the grief of a mother who has lost a child, or the anguish of the wife of an alcoholic, or the depression of the businessman who has just lost everything he had, including his dreams? I'll tell you: the person who has been through it.

If you have endured the cruel weight of loneliness, if you know what it's like to cry for help and love with no one to hear, then you have a special place in the family of God. You are a select counselor. God can use you to reach out to other lonely people.

When we suffer, God comes alongside us to comfort us in our darkness. When others suffer, then we can come alongside them as agents of God's healing power and love. Because such a ministry is open to us, we can have the confidence that our suffering, our loneliness, is never in vain.

If you are a child of God, if you have a personal relationship with Jesus Christ, then the Spirit of the Lord is upon you. You have been anointed by God to share the good news of Jesus Christ, to heal the brokenhearted, to proclaim liberation to those who are captives of loneliness and pain and sin, to join in a celebration with the family of faith.

Jesus is beside you. You are never alone.

10. THE LAST ENEMY

The Christian's Consolation in Grief and Death

The last enemy to be destroyed is death....When the perishable has been clothed with the imperishable, and the mortal with immortality, then the saying that is written will come true: "Death has been swallowed up in victory" (1 Cor. 15:26,54 NIV).

The Jaeger family's cabin cruiser rose and fell on the surface of the Atlantic Ocean. It had been a good day of deep-sea fishing for George Jaeger, his three sons, and his father. Despite the strong, brisk breeze and the gathering clouds, the day had been mild and the sea friendly, yielding a good catch.

Toward evening, however, the wind grew stronger, and the sea rose ominously. George Jaeger knew how to read the warning signs of the sea. With respect for the power of the elements, but without fear, he nosed his small craft toward home. Suddenly, the boat's engine sputtered, died, and refused to start.

The storm grew angrier. The sky darkened, and the waves rose to heights of ten feet and more, pounding over the sides and swamping the boat. A relaxing fishing trip had rapidly become a thing of horror.

George Jaeger calmly, efficiently, tied a rope through the laces of the lifejackets, tying himself, his father, and his sons together. As their small boat broke apart and sank beneath the crashing waves, the Jaeger men and boys bravely committed themselves to the Atlantic Ocean.

Together they struggled, straining to stay alive, but losing strength and hope. First one son, then a second, then a third drowned. Finally Grandpa Jaeger, weary from the struggle and choking on the sea water, gave up the fight and disappeared beneath the waves.

Eight hours later, George Jaeger staggered ashore alone, pulling the rope which still was attached to his three sons and his father, all dead.

Months after surviving this horror at sea, George Jaeger was able to say, "My youngest son Cliff was the first to go. I had always taught our children not to fear death, because it meant being with Christ. Cliff was a little boy, and he fought and fought the waves. The last thing he said to me was, 'Dad, I'd rather be with Jesus than to go on fighting anymore.' He died quietly with courage and dignity" (quoted in *The Effective Father* by Gordon MacDonald).

How will you face your death? Can you face it with the calm courage and hope of young Cliff Jaeger?

Character for a Crisis

Death is the last enemy of everyone on earth. But is death an enemy to be feared? Not for the person who has put his trust in Jesus Christ. Jesus came to destroy death's power and to free us from our slavery and fear of death. "In Him was *life*," wrote John, "and the life was the light of men" (1:4, italics mine). Jesus dispells our darkness, casts out our fear, makes us whole, and enables us to face life and death with triumphant courage and hope.

You can't truly be ready to live until you are ready to die, until the matter of your eternity with Christ is finally settled. There is a kind of courage and abandonment for the one who comes to terms with his death. Once you have received Christ into your life and have experienced emotionally as well as intellectually the realization that you will never die, then the fear of death has no ultimate power over you. Death has been swallowed up in victory.

One of the most comforting passages in the Bible is that of Revelation 21:3-4, in which John discloses his prophetic vision of a time beyond the grave, when "God will wipe away every tear" and "there shall be *no more death, nor sorrow, nor crying*; and there shall be *no more pain*, for the former things have passed away" (italics mine). This is the assurance that God has given us in His Word—an assurance that encourages us and enables us to really live.

A common denominator of all those who have been used in a great way for God is this: all had come to terms with death. The last enemy was no terror to them. They were confident of their eternal life with Christ. Their lives were hidden with Him.

Andrew Melville, who could speak for scores of Christian martyrs through the centuries, looked down at a crowd of onlookers and executioners before being burned at the stake for his faith, saying, "It matters little to me whether I burn in the air or rot in the ground! Do you think you can burn up the truth? I belong to Jesus!"

Jim Elliot, shortly before his martyr's death at the hands of the Auca Indians, said, "Be sure that when your time comes to die that all you have to do. . .is die." In other words, get your house in order now. Build Christian character into your life now, because people almost always die in the way they have lived.

If you're just drifting through life, denying the real issue of obedience to Jesus Christ and ignoring that inevitable event called death, then you're not preparing yourself for those crises that will certainly come. That preparation comes only through time spent in the Word of God, and in prayer, and in fellowship with your brothers and sisters in Christ. If you are not building that character into your life right now, then how will you cope when the storms come?

The Battle Against Death

Death is your enemy, even if you are a believer in Jesus Christ, even if you have the assurance that after death you will go home to be with Jesus. Death is the price paid by all of Adam's race for their disobedience to God's law. "The wages of sin," wrote Paul, "is death" (Rom. 6:23). This means both spiritual death (eternal separation from God, from which Jesus has saved us) and physical death (which all of us must face one day). Jesus Christ came into the world for this very reason: to destroy the great enemy of the human race, death.

Death was the enemy of Jesus Christ in His earthly ministry. In fact, the battle against sin and death *was* Christ's ministry on earth. As the Scriptures tell us, the Son of God was made flesh and shared in our humanity so that "through death He might destroy him who had the power of death, that is, the devil, and *release* those who through *fear of death* were all their lifetime subject to *bondage*" (Heb. 2:14–15, italics mine).

Are you enslaved by the fear of death? Jesus Christ wants you to know that death is an enemy that He has faced, battled, and defeated on the cross. He has broken the power of death and freed us from the slavery of its fear. How did Christ defeat death? Not by soaring over it, circumventing it, or denying it, but by going through it. Jesus Christ—the Son of God, the Son of man—was afflicted by the same sorrow, grief, and anguish that deeply wound us in the tragic times of our lives.

The Five Stages of Dying

My friend, a pastor in another city, was awakened late at night by a phone call—a death-call, in fact. The voice on the other end of the line told him the shocking news that Bob, a close friend and a member of his church, had died suddenly of a massive heart attack. Bob was only in his forties. No one would have guessed he could die so young, so suddenly.

This pastor's mind and emotions were in turmoil as he made the journey that night to Bob's home. What would he say to Jane, Bob's widow? On arriving, as he made his way past the many friends who had gathered at the home, he noticed the superficiality of the conversation around him. Finally he reached the place where Jane stood, and they embraced. Then Jane said to my friend, "Pastor, they won't let me talk about him! They won't let me talk about Bob, or about his death! I really believe they're more afraid of his death than I am!"

Death often comes without warning, a grim reaper, no respecter of persons. When death invades, we submit. Bob's friends couldn't face this fact. That feared subject—so long suppressed and sublimated by denial and activity—was suddenly, inescapably thrust before them. Bob and his friends were contemporaries, equals in age and health and status. They knew that what had happened to Bob could happen to them, so they refused to talk about it.

Elizabeth Kubler-Ross, in her book *On Death and Dying*, details the results of some two hundred interviews with terminally ill patients. She talks with these men, women, and children forthrightly, as they live in the shadow of fast-approaching death. Based on her research, Dr. Kubler-Ross presents five stages that many people pass through when they know they are going to die.

Stage One: Denial. The typical response of a person who discovers his life will end sooner than he imagined is that he denies it. "This can't be true. The tests are wrong. It can't be happening to me. I refuse to believe this."

Stage Two: Anger. We move from *"Not me!"* (denial) to *"Why me?"* (anger). Sometimes the anger takes the form of harsh bitterness. At other times it appears as a desire for total isolation. Whatever form it takes, this anger has to be worked out as the person moves through the process of dying.

Stage Three: Bargaining. After facing his anger, the patient often responds with a prayer like this: "God, if I'm going to have to die, could You give me six more months so I can see my daughter graduate from high school?" Or, "God, if You'll remove my disease or move it into remission, then I'll serve You with more zeal than ever before. I'll be more loving, more gracious, more obedient."

Stage Four: Depression. When the bargaining doesn't work, the patient often slumps into a time of deep emotional darkness. Tragically, many people undergoing the process of dying never move out of this stage. As a pastor, one of the saddest experiences for me has been to visit many dying people who never go beyond this stage. You may have been through that experience too. The final days or weeks or months of a loved one's life are spent in this stage, and his or her life is ended in deep darkness and bitterness.

Stage Five: Acceptance. In many cases, however, a person is able to work through his emotions to a place of acceptance. For the Christian, it is coming to the point of saying, "I am at peace, Lord. I surrender to Your will. I am ready to meet You." Perhaps you have seen this in the death of a loved one; I have. It's an experience of visiting a dying person and coming away saying, "I went to minister to him, and he ministered to me!"

These same five stages take place, not only in the emotions of the one who is dying, but very often with the loved ones who stand by the dying patient. In fact, these stages often take place with those who are going through a divorce, particularly with the one who did not initiate the divorce. And very often a person goes through these same stages upon discovering the infidelity of a spouse or a fiancée.

God Shares Your Grief

Sometimes we hear wonderful stories about someone who gently passes away with a prayer on his lips and a look of peace in his eyes, but it's not always that way, and we know that. Death is an enemy—so strong an enemy, in fact, that it took nothing less than the sacrifice of God's only Son to win the victory over death.

Joe Bayly, writing in his book *A View From The Hearse*, tells us that when his five-year-old son died of leukemia, his last experience with his little son was watching him as he was writhing in pain, hemorrhaging, crying out for a bedpan. Picture, if you dare, this beautiful little five-year-old child in such mortal agony—and then this precious child died, and Joe Bayly had *no* little boy. "How do you even begin to put into words how you feel?" he writes, of a sorrow, a groaning too deep for words.

Joe Bayly lost another son, this one at age eighteen. After a long period of grief and healing, he tried to put into words what he felt. In a passage from his book, *Psalms of My Life*, he wrote,

> What waste Lord
> This ointment precious
> Here out-poured
> Is treasure great

Beyond my mind can think.
For years
Until this midnight
It was safe
Contained
Awaiting careful use
Now broken
Wasted
The world is poor
—So poor
It needs each drop
Of such a store.
This treasure spent
Might feed a multitude
For all their days
And then yield even more.
This world is poor?
It's poorer now
My treasure is lost...

These are a father's honest feelings of grief in the face of incomprehensible tragedy. He loved and nurtured and cared for a son for eighteen years, and in one senseless moment that boy's life was poured out, gone, wasted. The doubt and pain and sorrow—and yes, the anger—of such a transcendent catastrophe are incomprehensible to someone who has never experienced such a loss. But God can comprehend this father's feelings, because He, too, has known the death of a Son. God doesn't rebuke Joe Bayly for those feelings.

Hebrews 4:14–16 tells us that Jesus is our "High Priest," fully God and fully man, made like us in every way—yet without sin. Because He became like us, He is able "to sympathize with our weaknesses." Therefore, we can confidently approach the throne of grace with all of our deepest feelings—grief, frustration, doubt, depression, heartache, even anger—and we know that there we can "obtain mercy and find grace to help in time of need."

One incident that shows how deeply Jesus felt about death is the story of the raising of Lazarus, found in the beautifully rich and moving eleventh chapter of the Gospel of John:

> Now a certain man was sick, Lazarus of Bethany, the town of Mary and her sister Martha. It was that Mary who anointed the Lord with fragrant oil and wiped His feet with her hair, whose brother Lazarus was sick. Therefore the sisters sent to Him, saying, "Lord, behold, he whom You love is sick." When Jesus heard that, He said, "This sickness is not unto death, but for the glory of God, that the Son of God may be glorified through it." Now Jesus loved Martha and her sister and Lazarus. So, when He heard that he was sick, He stayed two more days in the place where He was. Then after this, He said to the disciples, "Let us go to Judea again. . . . Lazarus is dead. And I am glad for your sakes that I was not there, that you may believe. Nevertheless let us go to him."
>
> Now Bethany was near Jerusalem, about two miles away. And many of the Jews had joined the women around Martha and Mary, to comfort them concerning their brother. Then Martha, as soon as she heard that Jesus was coming, went and met Him, but Mary was sitting in the house. Then Martha said to Jesus, "Lord, if You had been here, my brother would not have died. But even now I know that whatever You ask of God, God will give You." Jesus said to her, "Your brother will rise again." Martha said to Him, "I know that he will rise again in the resurrection at the last day." Jesus said to her, "I am the resurrection and the life. He who believes in Me, though he may die, he shall live. And whoever lives and believes in Me shall never die. . . ."
>
> Then, when Mary came where Jesus was, and saw Him, she fell down at His feet, saying to Him, "Lord, if You had been here, my brother would not have died." Therefore, when

Jesus saw her weeping, and the Jews who came with her weeping, He groaned in the spirit and was troubled. And He said, "Where have you laid him?" They said to Him, "Lord, come and see." Jesus wept. Then the Jews said, "See how He loved him!" And some of them said, "Could not this Man, who opened the eyes of the blind, also have kept this man from dying?"

Then Jesus, again groaning in Himself, came to the tomb. It was a cave, and a stone lay against it. Jesus said, "Take away the stone." Martha, the sister of him who was dead, said to Him, "Lord, by this time there is a stench, for he has been dead four days." Jesus said to her, "Did I not say to you that if you would believe you would see the glory of God?" Then they took away the stone from the place where the dead man was lying. And Jesus lifted up His eyes and said, "Father, I thank You that You have heard Me. And I know that You always hear Me, but because of the people who are standing by I said this, that they may believe that You sent Me." Now when He had said these things, He cried with a loud voice, "Lazarus, come forth!" And he who had died came out bound hand and foot with graveclothes, and his face was wrapped with a cloth. Jesus said to them, "Loose him, and let him go" (John 11:1-7,14-15,18-26,32-44).

Jesus Waited

John 11 depicts a dilemma with which we are all familiar: Shall we trust God—or face the facts? Notice that Jesus did not go to Lazarus immediately, even though He was deeply moved, even though He deeply loved Lazarus and his sisters. He had a deeper purpose for this event, so He waited two days before He began the journey to Bethany, and while He waited, Lazarus died.

Why does Christ sometimes delay in answering our requests? We've all felt that at times, haven't we? Why does He put off what seems (to us) to be a better plan? To Mary and

Martha, it would have been far better had Jesus come immediately to Lazarus, before he died. Why did He delay?

There are two reasons given in the text for Christ's delay: (1) "that the Son of God may be glorified" (v.4), and (2) "that you may believe" (v. 15), that is, that our faith might be strengthened.

Would you ever grow in faith if you immediately received everything you prayed for? A waiting time is a strengthening time, so that we can become conformed to the image of Jesus Christ. What have you been asking the Lord to do in your life? Does it seem as if He is delaying in answering your prayer? Biblically, this time is for character-building, for the building of your patience.

I don't mean to sound glib about this; this advice is not easy to give—or to take. I recall many occasions when my timing did not match God's timing at all. I became impatient with God's delay in answering my prayer, and I have questioned Him often. There have been times of worry and doubt and crisis in my life, times when I've anxiously prayed for a resolution and an end to my anxiety. But in retrospect, I almost always can see that God's timing was best. And when the wisdom of His timing is still not apparent, I just have to confess that I see "through a glass darkly."

God's ways are not man's ways. His timing is not our timing.

There are two different perspectives—human and divine —for every occurrence in life. The human perspective seeks to dictate God's timing and His means of bringing about healing. All too often, we act as though faith means telling God what to do. Ironically, in many quarters of the church, we are taught that the Christian perspective is to name and claim what we want, when we want it. No, that is human perspective. It's man-centered, not God-centered.

The divine perspective lets God be God. It trusts God's

love and surrenders to His sovereignty. It's the much harder of the two perspectives. It requires much more character, and an incredible amount of faith. It requires tremendous patience. But it is the biblical perspective; it's the truth.

Do you know the American prayer? It goes like this: "Lord, please give me more patience...*right now!*" It's hard for people who have been brought up on freeway express lanes, instant replays, Big Macs, Minute Rice, and Tang to simply *wait.* But Psalm 62:1 says, "My soul silently waits for God...." And Isaiah 40:31 says, "Those who wait on the LORD/Shall renew their strength...."

Understand the depth of that word *wait.* In the original Hebrew, to wait literally meant "to twist or be stretched in order to gain strength." Right now you may be waiting on the Lord's response to your prayer. I would encourage you to see that this waiting time is a stretching time so that you might grow strong. We grow strongest and learn the most not when things instantly come our way, but when we are required to wait.

Jesus knew that. Mary and Martha needed to know that. So do we.

Jesus Understood

When Jesus arrived in Bethany, He found Mary and Martha in a state of crisis, grief, and hopelessness. In fact, I would suggest that perhaps Mary and Martha were in the second stage of death-acceptance that Dr. Kubler-Ross describes: anger. I think they were expressing disillusionment and resentment when Martha said to Jesus, "My brother's in the tomb. He's been there four days. If You'd been here, he would've lived! Where *were* You? You delayed. You made us wait. You let us down."

Notice that Jesus didn't rebuke Mary and Martha for their

anger. Rather, He heard them out, then gave them this calm assurance: "Your brother will rise again." I'm deeply moved over Jesus' loving response. Not a rebuke, just a promise.

Perhaps Jesus took Martha's head into His arms and held her close to His chest, embracing her and saying, "I am the resurrection and the life. He who believes in Me, though he may die, he shall live, Martha. And whoever lives and believes in Me shall never die. Lazarus will not die, Martha" (vv. 25–26 author's paraphrase). I believe there is a tenderness here that the hurried student of the Word of God fails to picture. I think the Lord Jesus understood her feelings. He wanted her to work through her grief, her depression, her anger.

And just as He was with Mary and Martha, so He is with us.

For many of us, there is a deep inner reservoir of hurts, anger, denial, and depression; we've put a lid on those feelings so that we no longer believe it's okay for a Christian to share his brokenness at a time of grief. You may be holding back tears and feelings that need to be released, but for fear of being seen as weak or unspiritual, you don't shed those tears, you don't voice those feelings either before God or before other Christians. But the Lord wants to hear those feelings; He wants you to know it's okay to feel like that.

Jesus Wept

After Jesus had spoken with Martha, He waited outside the village of Bethany while Martha went back home to call her sister. When Mary heard that Jesus had come, she went to Him, fell at His feet, and said the same words as her sister, "Lord, if You had been here, my brother would not have died" (v. 32). And when Jesus saw Mary and Martha and their many friends weeping, the Gospel account says that

Jesus "groaned in the spirit and was troubled" (v. 33). The word *troubled* in the English doesn't begin to get at the full meaning in the Greek. It literally means a groaning too deep for words.

Jesus groaned within Himself, feeling the combined weight of His own grief and the grief of those around Him. "Where have you laid him?" Jesus asked (v. 34), and they led Him to a place within sight of the tomb of Lazarus. And there, says John 11:35, "Jesus wept."

Jesus wept!

How many times we've heard this verse lightly written off with the question, "What's the shortest verse in the Bible? Oh, yes, John 11:35, 'Jesus wept.' "

Yes, it's the shortest verse. It's also the deepest verse! The Gospel of John shows us Jesus Christ, the God-man, fully divine yet fully human, the omnipotent Creator-God in the flesh, feeling the loss of His friend, grieving with the family and friends of Lazarus in their heartache.

And He *wept!*

"See how He loved him!" said the other mourners (v. 36). And again John adds that Jesus was "groaning in Himself" (v. 38). Even though Jesus knew of the resurrection power within Him, even though He had already told Lazarus's grieving sisters, "Your brother will rise again" (v. 23), Jesus' grief for His beloved friend was achingly real. Jesus knew that Lazarus had tasted death; He knew better than anyone what the awful reality of death was because He had come to do battle with death. Jesus' heart was broken. His example and His tears hallow and sanctify the expression of human grief.

In Romans 12:15, Paul wrote, "Mourn with those who mourn" (NIV) or, in another translation, "Weep with those who weep" (NKJV). A modern paraphrase of 1 Thessalonians 4:13 might read, "Brothers and sisters, I want you to understand that it's okay to weep over your lost loved ones. Just don't weep as those who have no hope." Our hope is in the One who raised Lazarus. Our tears and feelings of grief are sanctified by the example of Jesus Christ and by the words of the apostle Paul.

Jesus Christ stands beside us in our times of deepest grief and doubt and pain. He is touched with all our feelings and questions. Jesus' attitude toward death is reflected in His words and deeds and prayers prior to His own death on the cross.

We see in the Gospels that death stalked Jesus throughout His ministry, and toward the end of His life we see that Jesus dreaded His own approaching death. The Gospels speak clearly and poignantly of Jesus' agony in the Garden of Gethsemane. Matthew 26:37–39 depicts Jesus in the throes of deep depression:

> He took with Him Peter and the two sons of Zebedee, and He began to be sorrowful and deeply distressed. Then He said to them, "My soul is exceedingly sorrowful, even to death. Stay here and watch with Me." He went a little farther and fell on His face, and prayed, saying, "O My Father, if it is possible, let this cup pass from Me; nevertheless, not as I will, but as you will."

Mark 14:33–34 draws a similar picture: "He [Jesus] began to be troubled and deeply distressed. . . . 'My soul is exceedingly sorrowful, even to death,'" He said. And in Luke 22:41–44, Jesus

> knelt down and prayed, saying, "Father, if it is Your will, remove this cup from Me; nevertheless not My will, but Yours, be done." Then an angel appeared to Him from heaven, strengthening Him. And being in agony, He prayed more earnestly. And His sweat became like great drops of blood falling down to the ground.

This anguish is beyond our ability to imagine! Was Christ fearful of being dragged to a horrible and unwilling death? No, that's not the picture of Jesus in the Gospels. True, He did not want to die—He asked the Father, if at all possible, to take the cup of death from Him—but He was obedient to the will of the Father, obedient to the death. Jesus knew the price He must pay, and He paid it voluntarily. "Not My will, Father, but Yours be done."

Clearly, Jesus wished that He could escape this death, much as each of us would wish to avoid the cold touch of that last enemy. But the special dread and anguish of this death lay not in normal human fear, or even in the terror of that hellish instrument of Roman execution, the cross. What Jesus obediently faced, with untold dread and unfathomable courage, was nothing less than the crushing, incalculable burden of the entire world's suffering and sin—yours and mine. He knew that when the hour of His death came, the full and awful weight of our sin would fall upon Him, and the sacrificial Son of God literally would be blotted out of the sight of God—cut off, separated from the Father with whom Jesus had eternally been one.

The Book of Hebrews tells us that God made everything subject under Jesus; yet "at present we do not see everything subject to him. But we see Jesus, who was made a little lower than the angels"—when He emptied Himself of His prerogatives as God and obediently became flesh and blood like us—

now crowned with glory and honor *because he suffered death*, so that by the grace of God he might *taste death for everyone*. In bringing many sons to glory, it was fitting that God, for whom and through whom everything exists, should make the author of their salvation perfect through suffering. Both the one who makes men holy [that's Jesus] and those who are made holy [that's us] are of the same family. So Jesus is not ashamed to call them brothers (Heb. 2:9–11 NIV, italics mine).

What an astounding thought! Because He has suffered, because He has tasted death for us, Jesus Christ—the Son of God, the Son of man—is our brother, and God—His Father—is our Father. If you have a saving relationship with God, if you have made Jesus Christ your Lord and Savior, then He has made you His brother or sister.

The deciding issue is faith. I've observed again and again that the word *faith* means different things to different people. I believe the various understandings of this word can be separated into three categories. Two of these kinds of faith are defined by our culture; the third is defined in the Bible.

The Three Faiths

First, there is *intellectual faith*. Many of us have intellectual faith—the kind of faith whereby we give assent in our minds to a creed, a doctrine, a set of religious rites. We believe that Jesus lived and died, that He rose on the third day. We believe all the great doctrines of our denomination. It's part of our heritage. It's how we were raised. "I believe," we say. "I have faith." I want you to know that intellectual faith is not the faith of the kingdom of God; it will not save you. Have no illusions; intellectual faith will not redeem you from your sin or assure you of eternal life with Jesus Christ.

There is a second kind of faith that I call *temporal faith*. That is the kind of faith whereby we believe in God, we believe He is good and loving and benign, and that He's watching over us from above. He cares for us, our families, and our businesses, and we invoke His name when we open community meetings and football games. That is well and good, but temporal faith is not the faith of the Kingdom either; it will not save you or redeem you or assure you of eternal life.

There is a third kind of faith, which I call *redemptive faith;* I call it that because the Scriptures call it that. Redemptive faith involves surrender to God's kingdom; it means surrendering our possessions, our lifestyle, our family, our will, our entire life to Jesus Christ as *Lord* (not just as Savior!), and becoming citizens of the kingdom of God.

I want to be honest with you about this. It's my deep conviction that the majority of people who call themselves Christians operate only on the basis of intellectual faith or temporal faith, and sadly fail to understand what redemptive faith is all about. It doesn't matter whether you list yourself as Protestant or Catholic, Presbyterian, Baptist, Methodist, Adventist, or Pentecostal. If you don't have redemptive faith, you are not redeemed; you will not spend eternity with Jesus Christ.

This may sound old-fashioned to you, but this is what the Bible clearly attests. And because the Bible is so clear on this—in fact, because the call to redemptive faith is the central challenge and theme of all Scripture—I want you to be just as clear on this. I want you to know that God is reaching out to you through Jesus Christ; He invites you now to respond in true faith, surrendering all that you are and all that you have to Him.

As you contemplate your own life, your own eternity, and indeed your own death, I want to share with you a story from *You Are Never Alone* by Charles L. Allen. This story articulates far better than I can what it means to live by redemptive faith, with an assurance of eternal life with Jesus Christ.

John Todd was born in the autumn of 1800. When he was

only six years old, both his mother and father died. Orphaned and alone, young John was moved ten miles away to be raised by his aunt. All his early years he grew up with this aunt, who loved him and cared for him as though he were her own son. John Todd later went to college and seminary, and finally entered the pastorate. In his mid-forties, word came to him that his aunt was dying and that she was very afraid of her approaching death. On her deathbed, she wrote him a letter expressing her fear, and she asked him what death and eternity would be like. He wrote back this letter to her:

It is now thirty-five years since I, a little boy of six, was left quite alone in the world. You sent me word you would give me a home and be a kind mother to me. I have never forgotten the day when I made the long journey of ten miles to your house. I can still recall my disappointment when, instead of coming for me yourself, you sent one of your servants to fetch me. I well remember my tears and my anxiety as, perched high on your horse and clinging tight to your servant, I rode off to my new home.

Night fell before we finished the journey, and as it grew dark, I became lonely and afraid. "Do you think she'll go to bed before I get there?" I asked anxiously. "Oh, no," the servant said reassuringly. "She'll surely stay up for you. When we get out of these woods you'll see her candle shining in the window." Presently we did ride out in the clearing and there, sure enough, was your candle. I remember you were waiting at the door, that you lifted me—a tired and bewildered little boy—down from the horse. You had a big fire burning on the hearth, a hot supper waiting for me on the stove. After supper you took me to my new room, you heard me say my prayers, and then you sat beside me until I fell asleep.

You probably realize why I'm recalling all this to your memory. Someday soon, God will send for you, to take you to a new home. Don't fear the summons, the strange journey, or the dark messenger of death. God can be trusted to do as much for you as you were kind enough to do for me so many years ago. At the end of the road you will find love and a welcome waiting, and you will be safe in God's care. I shall watch you and pray for you until you are out of sight, and then wait for the day when I shall make the journey myself and find you waiting at the end of the road to greet me.

None of us knows when that day will come for us. None of us knows when we will meet that last enemy. You may be young and healthy now, and that hour may seem far away from you (though it could come in an unexpected instant, even today). You may be facing that journey very soon because of an incurable illness, or just because of the accumulation of years. Or maybe you're about to say goodbye to a friend or loved one or your lifelong mate. Whatever your situation, it is urgent that this issue be settled now: Do you have the faith that redeems? Do your loved ones have this faith? How will you face your Last Enemy?

Death is our enemy, but what a friend we have in Jesus, who bears all our sins and grief. "The last enemy that will be destroyed," wrote Paul in 1 Corinthians 15:26,54, "is death. ...When this corruptible has put on incorruption, and this mortal has put on immortality, then shall be brought to pass the saying that is written: 'Death is swallowed up in victory.' "

Epilogue:
Tear-filled Eyes Can Still Focus on Jesus

Who shall separate us from the love of Christ? Shall tribulation, or distress, or persecution, or famine, or nakedness, or peril, or sword? ...Yet in all these things we are more than conquerors through Him who loved us. For I am persuaded that neither death nor life, nor angels nor principalities nor powers, nor things present nor things to come, nor height nor depth, nor any other created thing, shall be able to separate us from the love of God which is in Christ Jesus our Lord (Rom. 8:35, 37–39).

It was Easter, and the minister was delivering a sermon on the Resurrection. In the course of that message, the pastor posed this question: "Why did the women who visited the Lord's tomb not recognize Him? Why were they unable to see who Jesus really was?" And then, with conviction, he shared what he felt was the answer: "Because their eyes were filled with tears." The minister went on to apply this story to the needs of his congregation, saying that if we would see Jesus clearly, we must wipe the tears from our eyes and live a stoic existence, indifferent to our problems and struggles. I know this pastor sincerely meant well, but with all my heart I'm convinced he was wrong.

Tear-filled eyes *can* still focus on Christ.

In Psalm 6:8, David writes, "The LORD has heard the voice of my weeping." It's all right to feel the way you feel. The Lord hears your weeping; He wants to heal you, not hurt you. The Father in heaven understands your loss, your sorrow, and your pain; He has known the death of a Son.

Don't be afraid to cry to God. Don't be afraid to share your brokenness with others. In times of trial, struggle, and loss, our tears are often a necessary release, beginning the healing process, enabling us to become whole. Our tears often communicate to our brothers and sisters in Christ that we are in need of care and prayer and concern. Our eyes can still focus on Jesus Christ and His love for us, even though they are filled with tears. The Lord understands, and He's here, alongside you, grieving with you, feeling your pain.

It's like the little girl whose playmate's life was suddenly lost in an automobile accident. Though only six years old, this little girl knew her friend's mother was very sad. Filled with grief over her playmate's death, and love for the grieving mother, this child decided to walk down the block and visit her. She didn't know what she would say; she didn't know what she would do. She only knew that she had to go to her.

The little girl was gone a long time. When she finally arrived home late for dinner, her anxious parents met her at the door. "Honey, why are you so late?" said her father. "Where have you been?" asked her mother. "We've been so worried—"

"I'm sorry I'm late," the little girl answered. "I was with my friend's mother."

The father glanced up at his wife, then looked again at his daughter. "What did you say to her?"

"I didn't say anything," said the little girl. "I just crawled up in her lap and cried with her."

Whatever your burden, Jesus Christ is alongside you now, sharing that burden. He understands, and He weeps with you. He wants to touch you with His healing love.

Our sorrows and afflictions are like storm clouds that

darken the sky from horizon to horizon; grief seems to hide God's face from our eyes. Right now, we can't understand the process of our suffering, because the full light of understanding is not revealed to us on this earth; by faith we know the light is there, above those clouds, beyond our sight. But even in the darkness we can know that Jesus Christ is beside us, and—like the little girl—He's weeping with us, sharing our sorrow.

God has lovingly, patiently been teaching me a difficult lesson: if I am open to Him, He will build a quality in my life that I would have attained in no other way but by going through the trials. That quality is like refined gold; it's the purified precious metal of Christlike character.

James wrote,

> The testing of your faith develops perseverance. Perseverance must finish its work so that you may be mature and complete, not lacking anything. . . . Blessed is the man who perseveres under trial, because when he has stood the test, he will receive the crown of life that God has promised to those who love him. . . . You have heard of Job's perseverance and have seen what the Lord finally brought about (1:3-4, 12; 5:11 NIV).

Job himself testified of what the Lord brought about in his life: "When He has tried me, I shall come forth as gold" (Job 23:10 NASB).

That is the testimony of suffering Christian saints and martyrs throughout the centuries. It's the witness of the apostle Paul, of Dietrich Bonnhoeffer, of C. S. Lewis, of Jim and Elisabeth Elliot, of Joni Eareckson Tada, and of Karl Kassulke. It's a lesson I'm still learning. It's what the Lord Jesus wants you to know as He is bending over you now, grieving with you, full of compassion and mercy.

Not all of the circumstances of your life will be joyful or

happy. But Jesus is with you, ready to take even the worst circumstances of your life and transform them into gold for your life on earth, and for your eternity with Him.

Tear-filled eyes can still focus on Jesus.